I0189853

Spiritual Whispers to the Soul

A Poetry Collection

by Heather D. Wright

Courtesy of Colorful Spirit Publishing

Copyright © 2012 Colorful Spirit Publishing

Protected by freecopyright.org

ISBN-10: 098596331X

ISBN-13: 978-0-9859633-1-6

Published by Colorful Spirit Publishing

*(Self-Publishing Company Owner & Author,
Heather D. Wright)*

A Personal Note of Dedication

This poetry book is dedicated first and foremost to God because, without Him and the inspiration He has given me, I would not have been able to write this book at all.

I would also like to dedicate this poetry book to my mother, Barbara Wright, and my father, Odell Wright, as well as my sister, Amy Wright, whose constant love and support have guided me my entire life to keep the faith and believe in myself.

I would also like to dedicate this poetry book to all the other family members, special friends, and other great souls that have inspired me to believe in my dreams.

Preface

Spiritual Whispers to the Soul is my first collection of poetry published by my newly created self-publishing company, Colorful Spirit Publishing. This book has been in the works for quite some time now, and it reflects the very essence of my heart and soul. Just like so many people, I have endured some of the hardest times in my life and could not understand why God would allow me to struggle so much. Even though God has blessed me with a wonderful family, good friends, and abundance in terms of work and other opportunities, my path has not always been an easy one. As I look back over the history of writing these poems, I was inspired to write about so many different experiences God wanted me to go through. In fact, it has been through my struggles and the writing of these poems, that I have grown closer to God and become an even stronger spiritual soul.

It is my hope that, as you read my poetry collection, that you will find the spiritual strength you have been seeking to face hard times and to know that you are not alone. I promise you that there is a poem in this collection that covers so many aspects of human suffering, and yet through God's guidance, He helped me to discover through my own life lessons, how to convey my own spiritual truths to all of you as well as the valuable lessons I have learned along the way.

As you read Spiritual Whispers to the Soul, I truly do have faith that you will hear spiritual wisdom echoed through practical experiences as well as feel encouraged knowing that you are not alone in your struggles. My prayer is that these poems offer much faith, hope, love, inspiration, encouragement, and healing to your own soul that is in need for guidance. I also hope these poems help you embrace your own destiny and learn valuable truths on your own journey in life.

Enjoy, my friends, and keep the faith. These spiritual whispers echoed in the art of poetry I have come to love so much is for you.

Sincerely,

Heather D. Wright

11:11

11:11 as I watch the clock time completely unfold...
It's a voice from above saying it's time to let your strength never grow old.

11:11 as I struggle to see a time with a different message that's best...
I keep thinking there's a reason you appear to put my racing thoughts to rest.

11:11 has a mystic message warning me it is time to wake up...
I just stare at your numbers feeling the healing presence of your ticking touch.

11:11 jumps out at me from every clock in the room...
Its constant angelic heartbeat guide me to not give up so soon.

11:11 is the number that continues to direct my distracted attention...
The Universe just has a way of helping me break the chains of unhealthy suspension.

11:11 shines its light so boldly in the quiet of another long, sleepless night...
Somehow it knows I just need peaceful vibes to keep my energy strong and light.

11:11 keeps my eyes focused on its very own special, cryptic voice...
It encourages me to keep the focus and make the right choice.

11:11 comes ever so faithfully to greet me before I lay down to sleep...
It's the number of the Universe that promises to keep my soul so deep.

11:11 casts eternal shadows of lifelong protection...
The numbers resonate in my soul to accept life without worry or rejection.

11:11 whisper words of hope and continued glory...
They surround my soul with a loving inspirational story.

11:11 always lets me know God is there to guide my path...
His energy lives within the numbers that are the spirit guides keeping me on track.

A Forget-Me-Not Flower Just for You

A forget-me-not flower just for you...
To let you know that I've never forgotten you.

A forget-me-not flower just to say...
You are in my heart and thoughts everyday.

A forget-me-not flower to heal your pain...
To let you know the sun will conquer the rain.

A forget-me-not flower to comfort your tears...
To help you find strength in the midst of your fears.

A forget-me-not flower to lift your strife...
So that you will never give up hope in this life.

A forget-me-not flower to make you smile...
Because I want you to know you are truly worthwhile.

A forget-me-not flower to bring you back...
To help you stay balanced when all else seems off track.

A forget-me-not flower to bring you light...
Because there are times we all need courage through the darkest nights.

A forget-me-not flower for my friend...
Because I will trust you forever even after this life ends.

A forget-me-not flower full of great love...
Because God keeps our hearts and souls united from the Heavens above.

A forget-me-not flower just for you...simply because I miss you.

A Kindred Spirit's Dream

I was heavy hearted from living a life where everything seemed so up in the air…
I was having a hard time moving forward because my spirit felt suffocated by moments of despair.
I thought to myself maybe I can escape into a dream world and imagine the life I want to be…
So I closed my eyes hoping God would help me discover a brand new destiny.

In the midst of the silence of night I fell asleep with you on my mind…
I wondered if maybe we could find a way to connect with a loving rhythm that continues each time.
In my dream I could see you walking with grace through a meadow of lovely flowers…
When I saw you I knew immediately you and I were gifted with magical spiritual powers.

I was not sure I could reach you because I felt trapped by obstacles I could not get past…
Then I felt you reach for my hand with such a magnetic force that would always last.
You asked me to follow you because you wanted me to feel my life was not in vain…
I knew we were destined to walk together through all the hopeless days and misguided games.

We walked through this meadow where everything seemed at peace…
You kept holding my hand to let me know you could feel my heart being unsettled and not at ease.
I looked you in the eye and could see right into your beautiful soul…
It was like we had lived so many lives before this one that I could never think of letting you go.

As I looked around us there were birds that sat on trees flapping their wings with so much joy…
They knew we were meant to embrace the good times and share in each other's turmoil.
The more we walked hand in hand the more I knew that God was leading us together on this path…
With you by my side I knew I could forgive my past hurts and not worry about looking back.

As the sunny day in the meadow of flowers came to an end in my dream…
I did not want to wake up because in this dream world you were free to be with me.
All I can remember when I awoke the next day…
Is feeling the touch of your hand and your warm embrace not wanting me to go away.

I knew the next morning this was more than just a casual dream…
In the depths of my soul I could still feel the power of your intense love still connecting with me.
When I opened my eyes I thought how I can bring this vision into our real lives without worry.
All I could pray was that the energy uniting us would bring us closer to igniting our true love story.

A Mother Like You

From the time of conception, God blessed you with a special destiny...
As the months passed until the magic number of nine, you fell in love with me.

During times when carrying me might have made you feel very sick...
Even after the morning sickness passed, you whispered, no matter how you felt, "don't quit".

In the moments when you were so tired and hungry and wanted everyone to leave you be...
All you ever did was make sure you took your weariest moments just to nurture me.

In the long days and nights when I kicked you from inside your womb...
All you did was smile so beautifully, knowing you would hold me in your loving arms soon.

When my birthday arrived and you spent hours in long, difficult labor that I might be born safe...
In my small way, I prayed that God would give you a peace that everything would be ok.

As I entered this world crying from the top of my lungs out loud...
All I can remember through my tears was that you held me in your arms smiling so proud.

When everyone left the room and it was just you and me...
You held me so close that I knew our heart and soul connection was meant to be.

Through all the times you fed, bathed, and clothed me as an infant, I was always so pleased...
For there was nobody else that loved me so much to take that kind of care of me.

As I became a toddler and began to play...
You always made sure I was kept safe in the best of ways.

When I started school as a child ready to take on all that God meant for me to know...
There were times you read to me at night and told me stories that helped me really learn to grow.

As the days, months, and years passed and I began to grow into a teenager with moody ways...
You made sure that you kept me in line and helped me know right from wrong everyday.

When I graduated from my high school to begin a new journey into higher education,
You sent me cards and prayed for me to be able to stand strong in the midst of any kind of rejection.

During my times of growing up and spending long days trying to work and go to school...
You always told me to be careful who I called a friend and who I let love me too.

When my time in college came to an end and I began my working career...
I heard you praying to God to help me find success in my life with no fear.

Now that I am middle aged I long for the times you let me know you are there...
I ask God to whisper these words, "I love you mom and thank you that you always cared".

Happy Mothers' Day during every moment I breathe...because my love for you is for eternity.

An Angel's Energy Wishes for a Special Soul

I wish you an Angel of Faith and Strength...
To keep you walking firmly on the right spiritual wavelength.

I wish you an Angel of Hope and Light...
To give you wisdom to make good choices when things don't feel right.

I wish you an Angel of Determination and Courage...
To help you smile when all you hear is the word discourage.

I wish you an Angel of Enlightenment and Vision...
To keep you seeing clearly when your heart feels trapped and imprisoned.

I wish you an Angel of Solace and Peace...
To help you find time to embrace moments of emotional release.

I wish you an Angel of Trust and Understanding...
To help you clarify all of life's crazy misunderstandings.

I wish you an Angel of Freedom and Victory...
To set your fears free from hopeless misery.

I wish you an Angel of Friendship and Purity...
To help you embrace your own special soul identity.

I wish you an Angel of Harmony and Joy...
To help you feel balanced when others around you try to destroy.

I wish you an Angel of Security and Protection...
To keep you feeling safe when you become a victim of unworthy deception.

I wish you an Angel of Wellness and Good Health...
To keep you surrounded by an aura of spiritual wealth.

I wish you an Angel of Light and Liberation...
To set your spirit free from unhealthy temptation.

I wish you an Angel of Beauty and Creativity...
To help break the chains of desperate insecurity.

I wish you an Angel of Intelligence and Wisdom...
To give you a renewed lease on life with strength and vision.

And most of all I wish you the Angel of Unconditional Love and Eternal Life...
To embrace your soul deeply with loving energy every day and night.

An Angel's Faith that Would Never Quit

I'm the angel of light ready to embrace your soul...
I watch you from above hoping you will never let me go.

I'm the angel of peace hoping to light your way...
All I can think of is how I want you to welcome my love for you one day.

I'm the angel of joy sending rain of peace to calm your fears...
I can see through the facade of joy you portray to hide your secret tears.

I'm the angel of courage giving you the strength to fight...
I can always tell when you face so many long, sleepless nights.

I'm the angel of time wanting you to make the most of each day...
I feel you when things are not going well and you just want to run away.

I'm the angel of unity bringing you closer to your dreams...
I will always make sure the choices you make are much greater than they seem.

I'm the angel of smiles that can encourage you to face all of life's suffocating chains
I understand there will be times when you think you are too weak to overcome their pain.

I'm the angel of bright days that can really enlighten your path...
I can protect you with my armor from all this world's crazy wrath.

I'm the angel of new beginnings ready to help you take on this world...
I can feel your spirit drowning in the midst of this life's crazy turmoil.

I'm the angel of rainbows full of every color to give you direction...
I will make sure in every way you are surrounded by divine protection.

I'm the angel of change that sings in harmony with the shifting wind...
I let my cool breeze of kindness embrace your soul like a long, awaited friend.

I'm the angel of emotions that can make you feel like your life is true...
I will hold your hand through all the tough times and always be loyal to you.

I'm the angel of freedom ready to give you wings to fly...
I will set you free from your burdens so you will not be captured by the world's endless whys.

I'm the angel of a better path God wanted me to bring into your life...
I trust I can give you the courage you need to rise above your present strife.

I'm the angel that will not quit because I love you unconditionally so...
My heart beats in harmony with yours so that, near or far, I can never let you go.

An Eternal Silent Prayer from God to You

If you feel alone and lost, I want to say keep the faith no matter what.
If you feel nobody truly cares, please know I do.
If you want to escape life and never look back, trust me I understand.
If you think your life is meaningless, please know you are special.
If you have no hope, please know this too shall pass.
If you think you have no way out of your circumstances, just know anything is possible.
If you lack faith, just know that everything happens for a reason.
If you are troubled and confused, please remember I care for you always.

And you may ask, why I care enough to send this heartfelt prayer to you...

Just because you are very special...
Just because I want you to live a life of great purpose...
Just because when you smile, I know it touches someone's heart...
Just because when you wake up, I know you can face a new day with courage...
Just because you are a light in the darkness to others who feel lost and alone...
Just because even when you are upset, you always have high hopes life will get better...
Just because even when others let you down, you always learn from your mistakes...
Just because you see the best in others even when others tear you down...
Just because you try so hard not to give up even when you feel nobody around you cares...
Just because you make the most of everyday even when the odds seem against you...
Just because you are a treasure meant to brighten this world with your beauty and truth...
Just because...I simply love you.

An Intrigued Soul Seeker that Drifts into a Dream

As I sleep and drift into a dream, Dear God, can you hear me cry...

Chained...
I feel chained by disappointing circumstances that try to hold me down.

Conflicted...
I feel pulled in so many different directions that I'm not sure which path is meant for me to travel.

Confused...
I sit alone wondering if I will ever accomplish my dreams.

Depressed...
I feel so down that I wonder if there really is a reason to have hope.

Embarrassed...
I feel embarrassed that I keep getting older with very few successes to cherish as the days pass.

Exhausted...
I feel the weight of emotional turmoil drain the energies needed to keep me feeling truly alive.

Frustrated...
I find myself walking in circles trying to make sense out of things that are beyond my understanding.

Isolated...
I want to reach out to one person to comfort my struggling heart trying to find its way out of chaos.

Saddened...
I feel saddened that life seems to be full of negative energy and routine rituals that linger on forever.

Silenced...
I feel silenced by a world that wants me to be all things to all people when all I want to do is be
true to myself.

Trapped...
I feel trapped in a world that tries to drown out my need for peace in the midst of constant struggles.

As I sleep and drift into a dream, I feel God touch my hand and hear Him whisper sweet words to comfort
my wounded soul...

Delivered...
No circumstance is too challenging for Me to help you overcome.

Enlightened...
You have to trust that everything in life offers you different choices and paths so you can find the one best
for you.

Understood...
You have to keep the faith that one day all your dreams will come true.

Excited...
You have to know there will be hard lessons to learn, yet you will grow stronger through adversity.

Confident...
You do not have to feel embarrassed because you will be rewarded for all your hard work one day.

Refreshed...
You will be set free from all your turmoil when you have faith that you can endure the present pain to see there truly is a light that burns brightest even in your darkest moments.

Peaceful...
You will no longer feel frustrated because all those circles you have been running in will eventually lead to a path in your life that clarifies where you have been and where you are going.

Comforted...
You will never be truly isolated because as long as you hold onto Me, I will never let you go.

Enthusiastic...
You can feel true inner joy knowing that this too shall pass and that good karma will always outweigh the negative energies that are not strong enough to restrain your spirit.

Expression...
You do not have to remain silent because I created you and want you to be true to yourself no matter what anyone else may expect from you.

Freedom...
You will never be trapped by your pain because my unconditional love for you will always set you free, give you hope, and embrace your spirit with complete serenity for eternity.

As I sleep and drift further into a dream, I feel God healing my troubled soul, as He gently whispers the words my weary spirit longs to hear and so desperately needs, to face the next year with greater courage and strength.

An Open-Minded Soul Like You

You are the kind of soul that knows how to brighten the darkest day…
All you gotta do is just say hello and my frustrations just melt away.

You are the kind of soul that is never too busy to let me know how you are…
All you gotta do is drop me a text message that lets me know you are never too far.

You are the kind of soul that tells me the right words to stay encouraged…
All you gotta do is say the tough times drift away when I refuse to remain discouraged.

You are the kind of soul that can make me laugh when I really need a much needed break…
All you gotta do is just remain strong when all I wanna do is just escape.

You are the kind of soul that knows how to keep me grounded without losing control….
All you gotta do is free me from confusion so I know God will never let me go.

You are the kind of soul that can tell when something is not quite right…
All you gotta do is ask if all is well and if I can remain strong through my hardest nights.

You are the kind of soul that has a special way of taking the right kind of action…
All you gotta do is smile at me and let know all I need is a diversion from difficult reactions.

You are the kind of soul that is always faithful to the heart…
All you gotta do is just be there and I feel at peace right from the start.

You are the kind of soul that knows when it's time to laugh or time to mend broken fences…
All you gotta do is just help me not become a victim of helpless circumstances.

You are the kind of soul that I can count on through every season of life…
All you gotta do is just be true to me when my goodness is overcome by relentless strife.

You are the kind of soul everyone wishes he or she had for a trusted friend...
All you gotta do is just be there with a special spirit that remains faithful to the end.

An Understandable Soul's Cry to be Free

Have you ever heard a soul in pain cry for something to set it free...
There's a longing within its depths to escape continual misery.

Have you heard a soul crying for someone to listen to its pain...
This is a soul that needs a refuge from all of life's suffering and shame.

Have you heard a soul screaming for someone to embrace its weariness...
There are times some soul needs to be released from emotional dizziness.

Have you ever heard a soul desperate to be rescued from days full of frustration...
Every soul finds himself in a cage needing to be released from unending humiliation.

Have you ever really stopped to ask a wounded soul what is really wrong...
Sometimes a soul needs just one person to help him learn how to be strong.

Have you ever really wondered why a soul's eyes are drowning with tears...
Maybe this soul is eager to have someone understand and calm its raging fears.

Have you ever truly taken a hurting soul by his withered hand...
Sometimes that is all it takes for one soul to know you really understand.

Have you ever taken a chance to let a burdened soul know he is not alone...
It means the world to one soul to know you can lead him back to his true home.

Have you ever really listened between the lines when a soul tells you he needs you to be there...
Sometimes that is all one soul really needs to make sure you truly care.

Have you ever been given a song and it reminds you of one soul's need for direction...
Maybe it takes just a minute of time to let a soul know that you feel his imperfections.

Have you ever felt a longing within a soul so desperate to be set free from his worries...
All it takes is your dedication to help one soul face life's more enlightening stories.

Have you ever lay awake at night feeling a soul's emotional distress...
That could be a sign this soul really needs your healing touch and calming presence.

Have you seen signs that put you in synch with the thoughts that haunt a soul's mind...
God is leading you back to the soul that needs you to open its eyes so it does not feel so blind.

Have you ever felt so lost that you wonder where the other half of your soul could be...
Then you have a dream one night and realize you are the one that makes that soul truly happy.

Have you ever just felt your heart feeling such a deep, spiritual connection...
As the days and nights unfold, there is one lost soul crying out for your much needed protection.

Have you ever just come looking to rescue a lost soul from crying...
That will be the time your unconditional love will keep me from dying.

Beautiful Journey Taken by One Soul into the Sea

My soul was on a journey to find some much needed peace...
There was a spiritual calling from the Heavens to escape my life and find some emotional release.
As I journeyed into a crystal blue ocean sea...
I could feel God whispering let the water that surrounds you set your spirit free.

When I walked to the edge of the water, the waves greeted me with a cool touch...
It was like they wanted me to keep the faith and quit feeling like I am not good enough.
Curious to know what this ocean water had in store for me to learn...
I decided to swim into the water hoping to ease all the tension of life's unexpected turns.

Wave after wave came gently to refresh my wounded, weary soul...
All I could think of was how my past had taught me that sometimes you have to let go.
Every now and then I would completely go under the water to hear what the sea had to say...
It reminded me of all the moments in my life where I had to endure hardship and not run away.

When I would come up from the water to take a breath or two...
I could almost hear God whisper there is healing in this saltwater for you.
Sometimes I would just drift in the water feeling like I had nothing to secure my careless feet...
I just let the current of nature carry me further on the waves of courage and no defeat.

When I would get weary and felt I needed something to keep me strong and grounded in love...
I hoped the seashells I touched would keep be connected to God's protection from above.
As I swam back to the shore and looked back at the sun shining on the water that healed my heart.
I felt guided to thank God for giving me strength at all times to keep the faith and not fall part.

Drifting

I drift from left to right only to see you hoping I will come your way...
Yet I can't stand another moment when I become a victim to your endless false praise.

I drift another way to try and find some peace of mind....
I hear the words you say and realize it's just a moment of weakness where you pretend to be kind.

I drift to a place where I can seclude myself from endless moments of pain...
Sometimes I feel suffocated by a world of heavy, depressed chains.

I drift to the crowd hoping to get lost in the chaotic rush of constant chatter...
Yet my silent stance is just a cry for help from the moments that really don't matter.

I drift to my car hoping to take a ride away from everything causing my heart to break...
Somehow I drive in circles in what seems to be a desperate attempt to not suffocate.

I drift to nature to escape the anxious thoughts flooding the blood in my brain...
Yet I cannot seem to find that balance without leaning more to the world of challenge and shame.

I drift to a harmonious song that I think will take me away from my daily sadness...
Somehow there is a moment of peace that I wish would last in the middle of my relentless madness.

I drift to a sunrise that hopefully will enlighten my dark, isolated existence...
There has to be a time that the desires in my heart will be met with continued persistence.

I drift to a warm place to find comfort in the midst of a cold blizzard of constant snow...
In my heart I know your memory is the picture of hope that gives me courage to remain bold.

I drift to a shade tree to find some cool place to rest my weary soul from shifting sand...
The fallen leaves before me tell me that letting go is better than always trying to understand.

I drift from one place to the next desperately hoping to find a peaceful, spiritual place...
God whispers to look within and have faith that all that's broken will be restored one day.

Everyone Has a Light Inside

Everyone has a light of hope inside…

The kind that keeps him dreaming when wanting to forget.

Everyone has a light of love inside…

The kind that wants to connect with at least one person who understands you better than yourself.

Everyone has a light of truth inside…

The kind that wants to trust that what you feel and experience is always from the heart.

Everyone has a light of faith inside…

The kind that motivates him to keep believing life has purpose.

Everyone has a light inside that wants to keep burning when all hope seems lost…

Thank you for encouraging me to keep my light burning against all odds.

Facing the Crossroads of Life

I was standing at a crossroads trying to make up my mind...
I looked up into the Heavens and said God which way should I go this time?
There never seemed to be a clear cut answer to all of my plans...
God just whispered to me that maybe it was time I quit trying to understand.

I was facing a crossroads where choices were not easy to make...
I was scared to death my present decisions would be a repeat of my past mistakes.
Kneeling at the crossroads I decided to say a prayer to God above...
I first begged Him to show me the right path on which to walk with great wisdom and love.

With my knees on the ground and my head hung as low as could be...
I prayed with such faith that God would show the right path for me.
He said life is not always easy and sometimes it is hard to know which way to go...
But I gave you the power of free will so that whatever choice you make will help you grow.

With tears in my eyes I cried out Lord you know I am always messing up my life...
God said but think of all that you learned from the wrong choices that eventually turned out alright.
I said I know what you mean but why do I still feel like such a complete misguided fool...
He said you must quit beating up yourself because I have always had great faith in you.

I just lacked the faith in myself to make the best decision as this crossroads stared me in the face...
I said God I know you love me, but I always fear I will let You down and be your biggest disgrace.
It seemed I just could not find the inner strength to stand up and choose the right path for me.
God said trust in your instincts and follow your heart because it will lead you to your destiny.

For some reason I knew that there was a lesson to be learned as God talked to me at this time...
I knew somewhere in my gut instincts and deep in my heart that I had to leave the past behind.
As I took a leap of faith onto the path that seemed to be pulling my heart and soul its direction...
I could feel God send His energy of guidance and forever loving protection.

Leaving the crossroads was one of the hardest places I ever had to move past...
As I took every step forward I knew God was giving me a new journey built on a hope that lasts.
Sometimes I feel tempted to look back to see where I have been to figure out where this path leads...
Yet somewhere within my soul, I know God has given me courage to do my best with good deeds.

Faith

by Kristan Elizabeth Jenkins

Faith, first and foremost, is believing in God
Knowing that someone much greater than ourselves has a purpose for us,
if we only take the time to listen.

Yet, Faith is also believing in the beauty of life
Knowing that our lives are truly meaningful
That our successes and our failures, our suffering and our happiness,
our hard work and our dedication have a much greater meaning than we can ever understand.
Simply knowing that life has a way of working out for
the best even we are not aware.

Faith is believing in others
Knowing that God has sent other people into our lives to help
us through our sorrows
and to share our joys.

Faith is believing in ourselves
Knowing that we can love ourselves and make our dreams come true even after
we have acknowledged our strengths and accepted our weaknesses.

Faith is believing that we are a part of something much greater than ourselves
Knowing within ourselves that love, in the purest form, still exists.

I Wish I Wish

I wish I wish I could come back from this…
There is a hole in my heart that just seems broken and dismissed.

I wish I wish I could escape from my pain…
Yet there are so many struggles that never seem to let go of my good name.

I wish I wish I could just find the path to true joy…
But I can't seem to escape the world that has trapped me under constant turmoil.

I wish I wish I could just find a way to overcome my stress…
But the grip of darkness wants me to stay chained to a life of misery and great sadness.

I wish I wish I could find a better way to understand what I feel…
Every time I think I am ok I learn that maybe my wounded heart will never heal.

I wish I wish I could find some way to end all of my losses and regrets…
Somehow they just keep happening all the time that I cannot escape all the brokenness.

I wish I wish I could figure out a way to turn off the racing thoughts in my mind…
It seems to play the darkest tricks on me and can be unusually deceptive when I think its kind.

I wish I wish I could keep from hurting so much…
I feel I play the part of an injured soul trying to survive in a world where I feel so out of touch.

I wish I wish I could just find a way to end this unhappy life that I call home…
No matter how hard I try to be at peace, my inner spirit quickly fades from warm to cold.

I wish I wish I could just forget all the problems in my life…
It seems they all just keep playing the same old song to create a melody of constant strife.

I wish I wish…
Please God help me to survive the craziness.

I Wish to Let Go and Let God

I always thought I knew all the correct things to say...
Then when I fell to my knees God told me he would show me the right way to pray.
I always felt I could find my way out of any tough problem that tried to bring me down...
All I had to do was just keep the faith and let God give me a smile when the world made me frown.

I always wondered if I could just take care of all my problems the way I felt was best...
Then I could hear a heavenly whisper cry out I know how to ease your worries with peaceful rest.
I always tried to find the right path to a new beginning that I thought was wise...
But no matter how hard I looked for direction God used many things to catch me by surprise.

I always took long walks here and there to try and find how to make my dreams come true...
God always said if you will just trust me, I will make sure people are good to you.
I always tried to do things my way because I felt my way was the only way to be...
Yet I could walk outside and feel God shout You must learn to hold on to me.

I always swayed from one way to the other trying to do the best I can...
It was God who threw me a life jacket and said all is well so quit trying to understand.
I always searched high and low to try and find the best ways for life to make sense...
Somehow God provided the road signs that worked together without such tragedy and suspense.

I always asked myself why do I have to be the one who always comes in last...
God just grabbed my hand and said I love you and will make sure you overcome your past.
I always looked to everyone else to try and please them when I suffered in shame...
God said I know you are frustrated but lean on me and I will protect your good name.

I always felt like I was never good enough because I felt so insecure...
Yet God was the one who stood right beside me with His healing touch and miraculous cures.
I always spent so many nights crying so much because my life seemed so out of sync...
It was learning to let go and trusting God that helped me find the key to my true destiny.

Journey of the Heart

In this life there exists a journey...
For some this journey is one of great pain, reaching for something that may not ever happen...
For others this journey is one of great sorrow if you lose what you love...
For many people this journey is one of confusion, for the heart can take us through so many
twists and turns in life that it is hard to stay on the right track...
For this world this journey is one of false illusions and egotism disguised as a loving gesture...

For every man, woman, and child, this journey is special, yet often challenging...
For one man, this journey leads him to the love of his life...
For one woman, this journey leads her to the love of her life...
For one child, this journey leads him into the arms of a loving father and mother who long for
that child's special touch...
For all of God's special creatures, this journey leads to the unconditional love an owner has for its pet...

No matter what or who you are, this journey will bring you great surprises...
No matter what you think you deserve or don't deserve, this journey may bring you pain...
No matter what your status, there will be days you feel you are suffocating from disappointment...
No matter what your desire, there will be days when the highs of reciprocal love allow you to conquer
your deepest fears and embrace your greatest triumphs...
No matter where the journey of the heart takes you, the one constant that remains is love...

When true love is involved...through all the pain...through all the heartbreak...through all the
sorrows...through all the highs...and through all the lows...there will always be the heart longing for love
and refusing to fall victim to the uncertainties of this life because it has been captured by the true magic of
equal give and take.

In this life there exists a journey where the heart conquers the mind, where true love overcomes logic, and
where we can all reflect on the lessons we have learned in matters of the heart along life's way and just
thank God He loves us and lets us love others along our journey of self-discovery and great sacrifice just
to have the chance to say to another yearning soul those precious words, "I love you".

Just a Talk Between a Fallen Angel and God

The Fallen Angel cried, "Dear God, why could I not just stay in Heaven with You?"

God replied, "Because someone else needs you."

The Fallen Angel asked, "Why cannot I go back to be with You?"

God replied, "Because there is work to be done and you are my faithful servant to fulfill the task".

The Fallen Angel asked, "Why did you not choose another more experienced angel?"

God replied, "Because you have the biggest heart."

The Fallen Angel asked, "Why do I have the biggest heart?"

God replied, "You always cry when you look over the clouds and see someone hurting."

The Fallen Angel asked, "How do you know when I see someone hurting?"

God replied, "Because I see you shedding a tear wishing you could be there to hold that person's hand."

The Fallen Angel asked, "How do you know when I am crying?"

God replied, "Because I hear you weeping and wishing you could take that person's pain away."

The Fallen Angel asked, "How can I take anyone's pain away for I am just a servant in Your Eyes."

God replied, "Because of your humility, I have sent you away from Paradise to live in a world full of real chaos and pain."

The Fallen Angel asked, "How can I live in a world surrounded by all this pain and misery?"

God replied, "Because I see you struggle in your sleep with torment filled with dreams wondering how you can reach out to caress the wounded soul of another human being."

The Fallen Angel asked, "How do you know my dreams are filled with suffering?"

God replied, "Because I feel your energy and know you will not rest at peace until your life has touched another in such desperate need of angelic peace."

The Fallen Angel asked, "How can I touch another life when I am use to a life where there is no pain or troubles, when everything around me is always in complete harmony?

God replied, "Because I know you have the harmony within you to bring balance to the most unbalanced of places."

The Fallen Angel asked, "How can I bring balance when I lay here on the ground, broken and confused about my own life and my mission here on this Earth?"

God replied, "Because I know you understand the pain of others and can heal their wounded spirits."

The Fallen Angel asked, "But why me of all the angels?"

God replied, "Why not? Because now that you understand what it is like to fall from grace, you have the strength to help others rise above their own suffering to believe in themselves and embrace life again."

Keeping the Light Inside

Everyone has a light of hope inside…

The kind that keeps him dreaming when wanting to forget.

Everyone has a light of love inside…

The kind that wants to connect with at least one person who understands you better than yourself.

Everyone has a light of truth inside…

The kind that wants to trust that what you feel and experience is always from the heart.

Everyone has a light of faith inside…

The kind that motivates him to keep believing life has purpose.

Everyone has a light inside that wants to keep burning when all hope seems lost…

Thank you for encouraging me to keep my light burning against all odds.

Keep the Faith

Life can be so hard…

Yet you must not give up.

People can hurt you deeply…

Yet you have to forgive.

Family can disappoint you…

Yet you must know your ties of love will conquer the pain.

Friends may not be there when you need them most…

Yet you don't have to feel so alone.

Jobs come and go…

Yet you must not let it make you feel you are not talented.

Change will affect your life…

Yet you must embrace it with great enthusiasm.

Sunny days and stormy nights are inevitable…

Yet with every moment, you must know there is a reason for everything.

As the moments of life unfold, keep the faith that everything will be ok.

Losing You

I cannot imagine how lost you must feel.

Losing a loved one is never easy.

If I could put myself in your shoes, I would do it so you never have to feel so sad.

I know the one you lost meant so much.

And yet I know that as hard as it is to let go, the spirit lives on.

I am here for you and will always wish you the best in life.

Just so you know…you are not alone and I care for you very much.

Love Always

When I think of you, my heart beats with such strength within me…

I think of how lost I would be without you.

When I hear you speak my name…

I feel I am the only person in the world.

When you look into my eyes…

I see a world where truth and honesty reign.

When we walk beside each other…

I know God has blessed me with true love.

When I think of you, I feel blessed because you are the One for me.

Merry-Go-Round Battles

This merry-go-round never seems to stop...
It just keeps going on so strong that I feel I'm about to blow my top.

This merry-go-round spins and spins...
It seems like I remain the loser of my fate and someone else always wins.

This merry-go-round tries to pick up speed...
I'm begging it to stop so I can find the strength to breathe.

This merry-go-round seems to get me all confused...
The ones on the ride attack my heart and leave it broken and abused.

This merry-go-round is more than just a simple leisure ride...
It's the up and down carousel that wounds my integrity and pride.

This merry-go-round will not let my secret cries come to an end...
I just keep wondering if it will slow down long enough to keep me from losing my friends.

This merry-go-round is not meant for me to control...
I remain at the mercy of its relentless captain whose chains entrap my soul.

This merry-go-round just will not seem to quit turning...
I'm crying on the inside wishing my stomach would just quit churning.

This merry-go-round goes so fast I can barely tell the good from the bad...
All I can do is feel the part of me that always feels so deeply sad.

This merry-go-round keeps me in the most difficult state of mind...
All I want is someone to just love me for who I am without feeling I'm the giver all the time.

This merry-go-round will one day truly conquer my dreams and destroy my soul...
I just pray to God that He can help me find the courage to just let go.

My Never Ending Christmas Wishes

What I wish for Christmas is something most people seek to find...
An eternal hope from above that is more true than empty promises and constant lies.

What I wish for Christmas is a treasured jewel wrapped in a red box that is full of great promise...
Spiritual words from an angel freeing me from the people who are destructive and dishonest.

What I wish for Christmas is a box of candles hoping to find a home in which to shine their light...
A light that can pierce the darkness with great joy on all the cold, snowy winter nights.

What I wish for Christmas is a bed of roses where I could lay my mind to rest...
A soft place to fall to protect my mind from feeling lost in a world of unworthiness.

What I wish for Christmas are arms around my spirit telling me all will be ok...
An embrace so magical it can take me away from all my internal pain on my saddest days.

What I wish for Christmas is a hand of peace to keep me from making the same mistakes...
A hand so strong and warm that lifts me up when the worries of life keep me feeling afraid.

What I wish for Christmas are words of kindness to keep me from falling apart...
Words full of positive energy that will warm the soul and keep me from losing heart.

What I wish for Christmas is a small bird to greet me with wings of true, loving freedom...
Wings that can strengthen my soul to fly free when I fall victim to a world of drifting wisdom.

What I wish for Christmas is a box of colorful seashells from every coastal land...
A shell of security and strength to keep me feeling tough when it feels nobody really understands.

What I wish for Christmas is a special key to unlock my soul clouded by a path of confusion...
A golden key of faith that can free other trapped souls suffering in a world of disillusion.

What I wish for Christmas is a mirror that reminds me of all of the places I have been...
A mirror reflecting the past where I have lived and where I hope to find myself happy again.

What I wish for Christmas is a breath of fresh air to help me take in the purity of life...
An air so free of torment that I can breathe freely without clouds of smoke and strife.

What I wish for Christmas is a warm blanket to cover me up from the pressures of this world...
A blanket so rich in God's love that I will not have to keep suffering from my inner turmoil.

What I wish for Christmas is a new beginning to start off another successful year...
New fresh starts that will take me into the future with great courage and limitless fear.

What I wish for Christmas is a spiritual path leading me to the heart of a brand new song...
A melody so rich in harmony and love that I can survive life's challenges when things go wrong.

What I wish for Christmas comes from God above...its great spiritual treasures filled with love.

My Partnership to Depression

Once upon a time I became bound to someone named Depression...
He said if you keep clinging to me I will teach you a lesson.

When I took him by the hand I did not know what an emotional ride it would be...
But I held onto to his hand and found that within my heart all I could feel was misery.

There were times I thought I could even cheer him up...
Yet he always made he feel so down all I could think of was giving up.

Even when I attempted to look at him with a smile...
He just frowned at me and said my life was not worthwhile.

In moments of pain and my deepest distress...
All Depression would do is chain me to nights of sleepless rest.

When the sun would shine and I tried to get him to see the bright side...
He would say it is going to be a stormy and rainy day and just wanted me to hide.

As the months and years rolled by, I thought Depression would figure out I needed to be happy...
Yet somehow he would put me down and told me this world was my enemy.

I spent countless days trying to love him so much that it hurt...
All he could do is attack my spirit that I always felt lower than dirt.

There were moments in my heaviest of tears I cried out for him to let me go...
Every time I thought he agreed his answer was always "no".

I knew my life had been going up in flames since he and I had been together...
Yet he did not seem to care and hoped I would live with him in turmoil forever.

As I looked in the mirror and saw the tears in my eyes...
I saw in a distance Depression staring at me himself with his continual weary cries.

There were times I wondered why God would let me stay linked to Depression all these years...
I have prayed day and night to be released from his suffocating fears.

As I stared out my window for a small glimpse of a better day...
I looked up to Heaven and tried to find the strength to pray.

The world looked so dark that I could not ask God to free me from my pain.
All I could remember as I began to weep is seeing the sun fade into the rain.

I walked out the door on Depression hoping he would not find me...
Yet his draining emotional energy bound me to him relentlessly.

As I fell to the ground praying for God to save me...all I could feel was my last heartbeat fading.

Please Forgive Me

I am so sorry I hurt you.

If I could turn back time, I would take back the words that broke your heart.

I am so sorry I was selfish.

If I could just put myself in your shoes, I would understand your point of view so much better.

I am so sorry for letting you down.

If I could change what I did, I would do so in a heartbeat.

Even though I know I hurt you, please forgive me for breaking your spirit.

Spinning in Circles

I'm spinning in circles trying to find my lost way...
Maybe one of those soaring eagles that watches from above will carry me away.

I'm spinning in circles trying to answer all of life's whys...
Yet I find myself drowning in my sleep with my persistent cries.

I'm living on a merry-go-round that never seems to quit...
All I can do is pray out loud that my emotional exhaustion will keep giving me a fit.

I'm bouncing around from one daydream to the next hoping life will one day make sense...
Yet all of a sudden I find myself trapped a world of perpetual suspense.

I'm running from one path to the next to find something to soothe my pain...
But somehow my sadness clouds sunny days with shades of relentless rain.

I'm feeling every breath I take grow ever so weary...
And I know in my heart it is because I often feel so down and dreary.

I keep looking around for some way to escape all of life's unwelcome surprises...
I'm so tired of such stress that I find solace behind my daily disguises.

I'm thinking so many things I do not know where to start or end...
Yet all I know and need is the simple talk and comfort of a true, good friend.

I'm struggling everyday to climb over my mountains of despair...
And I try so hard to find protection under the wings of those I know really care.

I'm taking many risky detours every chance that I get...
And I keep hoping my choices will not result in some unwise and unwelcome bet.

I'm looking outside and inside for some shred of hope...
Yet I know God is always holding my hand when I'm just hanging on by a rope.

I'm turning pages of my calendar wondering if this day will be just like the last...
In my heart I long for the creative diversity of a life that surpasses my crazy past.

I'm listening to the clock tick with its usual, steady pace...
All I'm asking for is for something fresh and exciting to free me from my same old space.

I'm stretching my arms to embrace flocks of birds soaring clear, blue skies...
And just hoping I can find some level of serenity before I lose my breath and begin to die.

I'm spinning in circles just wishing my dreams would all finally come true...
And hoping my past state of turmoil disappears so the love of God can carry me through.

Spiritual Talks Between Some Seashells and Me

I was walking along a sandy coastal shore far from home...
When all of a sudden a blanket of seashells whispered we each have a story we want you to know.
I decided there was something spiritual pulling me to understand what each seashell had to say...
I knew in my heart I needed to walk this path and understand that this was going to be a special day.

As I walked a little further along the crystal blue ocean waves crashing on the shore...
A little broken seashell cried out I have been hurt but I keep dreaming and striving for more.
As I continued my journey I was greeted by a solid black seashell that seemed it had no friend...
It whispered thank you for taking the time to notice me when others kicks me into the sand.

When I walked a little more a purple and white striped seashell kept calling my name...
It shouted I once was part of a royal keepsake and have since been able to overcome great shame.
A little further on my path I noticed a solid white seashell that seemed to glow with joy...
It shared with me that its color of purity had given it protection from despair and turmoil.

I continued my walk when a yellow and orange seashell seemed to capture my eye...
It whispered I know how to bring tears of happiness to those who keep me close with time.
I was so intrigued that I walked further to find a red speckled seashell that seemed a little fearful...
It shouted I just need to know someone cares so the rough waves don't make me feel so dreadful.

I was then greeted by broken pieces of so many seashells I could barely understand their cries...
They all were telling me to not let the craziness of this world keep me buried under continual lies.
As I went a little further there was a curly brown seashell offering a crab a place to curl up inside...
It said there is always someone looking to keep us safe when we feel frustrated on the outside.

I could not believe all the different stories that each seashell had to share....
It was like they all wanted me to know that they were unique and still had a soul that truly cared.
As I came to the edge of the ocean water that embraced my weary feet...
A beautiful sand dollar washed up beside me to be my good luck charm to conquer life's defeats.

Spiritual Treasures

Sometimes life is so hard that you just think why I am here...
Many times you just want to quit because it feels you will never be able to conquer all your fears.
Sometimes it seems everything in your world is going just as you planned...
Then you find yourself lost in a world of false hopes where it is all you can do to understand.

In the still of night it feels your soul is heavy with grief beyond measure...
You find yourself praying for answers that will bring you much needed spiritual treasures.
As the darkness of night fades into a beautiful sunrise...
You face another day full of new fresh hopes and some kind of nice, welcome surprise.

During the long days when you are working so hard you wonder if you can make it through...
You find deep in your heart courage and strength guiding you through.
When you face the end of your day you wonder if anyone noticed your special existence...
Then a peace comes over your soul that helps you come to terms with all of the pain and resistance.

In quiet moments of the evening hours when the rush of daily life has come to a temporary end...
There are times you hope and pray that God will send you a much trusted friend.
When you look out the window to see the night fall once again and the moon shining bright...
You realize suddenly that the angels from Heaven are sending you a message that life will be all right.

During a night of dreams and mysteries that work to embrace your soul in a world of imagination...
This is the time God gave you to escape mundane moments and the trap of constant stagnation.
When everything seems so hard that the world just seems it will not stop making you sick...
The astral world of spiritual truth offers constant faith and love that will never quit.

Everyday we all struggle to find a place where we can endure the hard times that come our way...
It is with great faith in our hearts that we can look up for hope and ask God to help us as we pray.
No matter what setbacks attack us as we try to stand strong when negative forces hold us back...
All we have to do is keep holding on to the spiritual treasures that keep our hearts on the right track.

Spiritual Words of Wisdom from an Angel

I'm going to wrap my loving arms around you and never let you go…
I'll look down on you from the Heavens and give you joy and wisdom to help you grow.

I'm going to send you peaceful thoughts to calm your most challenged, crazy days…
I know there are times you need to know someone cares in the midst of uncertain ways.

I'm going to send sunshine to brighten your world in the midst of any distress…
When you lay your head down at night, I will give you serene thoughts and calm rest.

I'm going to whisper words of comfort when you just need to know someone truly cares…
Even when the world seems dark, I'll send a gentle breeze so you know I am always there.

I'm going to send you a song when you need to feel in complete harmony…
When the world seems cruel, I will color your world with an inspirational melody.

I'm going to come in your dreams when you need a visit from a friend who loves you much…
We can discover new treasures when the real world seems completely too hopeless to touch.

I'm going to fill your mind with visions of a nice, warm wave of unending devotion…
When everything seems chaotic, my heart will embrace your deepest of emotions.

I'm going to send a beautiful red bird your way to remind you that you are never alone…
No matter what the season, I will be there for you during all the times of hot and cold.

I'm going to send you a smile when you are driving to your destinations...
I know that when you feel lost I will guide you with great strength and dedication.

I'm going to walk beside you through every challenge you face…
I'll encourage you to stand strong and free you from life's miseries and inevitable disgrace.

I'm going to give you a special hug when you need to feel true warmth and connection…
I'll continue to love your soul, my friend, with divine and eternal inspiration.

Strength

When I need someone to dry my tears…

Your hand is always reaching out to comfort me.

When I want to feel a warm embrace…

I know I can count on you.

When I want to hear the words I love you…

I know that you always will say them without hesitation.

When I want to laugh, I know I am not alone.

When I feel life is almost too tough to endure…

All I have to do is smile and think of you.

When I need strength…I know you give me my wings to fly high.

Tears from a Soul Mate's Heart

In the dark of the night, I could feel you reach for my hand...
You could feel me crying on the inside hoping God would send someone who understands.
I listened for your voice calling out my name through every tear I have cried…
It was like you could feel the weariness of a soul grown tired with tough breaks and hard times.

I could walk to the mirror wondering the purpose for it all...
All I had to do was look behind me and I could see you catch me before I take a fall.
In much pain and sorrow I have fallen to my knees hoping to feel you by my side...
The harder I cried I could feel you place your arms around me to help get me through the night.

As I look out the window watching a little bird hanging from the feeder to nourish its soul...
I could feel you in its presence telling me to hold on tight to you and you would never let me go.
I walk outside thinking a walk will set me free from all the stress that seems to wear me down...
When I look up to the sky, I can see your spirit in an eagle flying telling me I'm not lost but found.

I could take a drive down a road to escape my crazy world that never makes sense...
Then you send me a lovely song filled with great peace and a much needed emotional release.
I could dream at night the most lovely vision of you coming to take me away...
It is like you can feel when I need to take a break from the worries of this life to find a better day.

When I face a new tomorrow with such fear that this day will be as sad as the last...
I feel you touch my heart with your warmth encouraging me to let go of the pain in my past.
As I work hard to try and get through another very hard night of feeling lost and confused...
All I have to do is say a prayer to God and He lets me feel the unconditional love from you.

I often spend all the money I ever had just to find a way to get closer to your soul…
When I have exhausted all my resources, I hear you say quit worrying and just have hope.
I wonder why God has allowed me to live this long without having all of you by my side...
Somehow He wanted me to know the pain of loss so I would know true love when it was my time.

Through all the tears I have cried I have asked God why life has to be so hard to endure...
In my pain I could feel Him sending your energy to help heal my sorrow with a heart that's pure.
I can close my eyes and create a new world where you and I no longer have to deal with our fears...
You are the spiritual love of my life that God gave to love me forever through all my heartfelt tears.

Tears from the Sky

Tears from the sky come falling down my way...
I raise my head up high and beg God to listen to me as I pray.

Tears from the sky fall like raindrops to the ground...
Angels try to protect my wounded heart as I fall helplessly to the ground.

Tears from the sky come rushing upon me so fast I cannot move...
I feel trapped in a world of stagnation shattered with false words and empty clues.

Tears from the sky are so powerful they truly entrap my misguided heart...
The lonely soldier in Heaven knows what it's like to have real love hidden by the dark.

Tears from the sky are so heavy I can hardly see what's right in front of me...
All I want to do is escape my meaningless existence into a world that's not drenched in misery.

Tears from the sky come refresh the brown grass that lies withered at my feet...
With each blade they shower I feel the weight of their lonely mist trapping me in defeat.

Tears from the sky at times are like a fine shower of welcome rain...
I wonder if the amount that falls is greater than my own tears isolating me in shame.

Tears from the sky often come in unbalanced waves and surprises...
The endless cycle of their journey reminds me of my constants fears and unexpected disguises.

Tears from the sky always seem to come at just the right season...
Their bittersweet dance comforts me when life's worries capture my spirit without reason.

Tears from the sky embrace the ones that come pouring down my face...
I feel it's one of God's angels telling me he understands what it's like to make troubled mistakes.

Tears from the sky enlighten my path as I learn to let go of all that keeps me so confused...
I kneel down with tears of hope asking God to give me strength and a love that's true.

Thanksgiving Prayer

Thank You for taking the time to tell me you truly care for me in my best and worst days...

Thank You for taking the time to let me know I am never really alone...

Thank You for taking the time to look into my eyes and see the very depth of my soul...

Thank You for taking the time to give me a simple hug just to let me know you are there...

Thank You for taking the time to let me see your smile on my most difficult days...

Thank You for taking the time to hold my hand when I need to know that everything will be ok...

Thank You for taking the time to really listen to me heart and soul...

Thank You for taking the time to walk beside me just so I know that someone else understands...

Thank You for taking the time to whisper in my ears sweet, comforting words to calm my fears...

Thank You for taking the time to be my friend when others let their own busyness consume them...

Thank You for just taking the time to be my everything...my guide...my protector...my leader...my true knight and shining armor because everyone needs someone, just one person that will truly love them heart and soul. To say thank You for all the special ways You have inspired me to be a better person, I want to say Thank You, and You know what God, now that You always take the time to do all these things for me...my prayer is that others will take the time to do this for those they truly love without regret and without letting another moment pass them by.   Thank You...thank You...thank You...my heart truly beats for You and in my dreams I know You are always there. I could not endure Thanksgiving without You for You are the true spirit of what Thanksgiving should be for all of us everyday of every season as the pages of our lives unfold and connect with You for eternity.

Thank You God for Friends

Thank you God for the day you brought me into this world...
Because of Your Divine Plan I'm blessed with friends who have helped me overcome my turmoil.

Thank you God for the friend who taught me that it was ok to smile...
This one helped me not to question whether or not my life was even worthwhile.

Thank you God for the friend who made me see it was ok to cry...
This one, through compassion, helped me realize all I had to do was just really try.

Thank you God for the friend who never stopped believing in me...
This one showed me my life was truly meant to be lived without misery.

Thank you God for the friend who was always there to make sure I was ok...
This one let me open my heart so someone else could know I was really afraid.

Thank you God for the friend who always knew how to cheer me up...
This one kept my spirit from falling apart when all I felt was completely stuck.

Thank you God for the friend who taught me what it was like to really trust...
This one showed me I was not always going to encounter consistent bad luck.

Thank you God for the friend who inspired me to always believe in my dreams...
This one showed me that life is not always what it seems.

Thank you God for the friend who let me never say never...
This one taught me to make a wish and hope that things would somehow get better.

Thank you God for the friend who could just look at me and know what was wrong...
This one told me that one day if I kept praying I would stop listening to life's hopeless songs.

Thank you God for the friend who never let a secret of mine become tainted with pain...
This one taught me that one day I could embrace life with true hope instead of feeling shame.

Thank you God for the friend who could always see that my life really was a gift...
This one proved to me that no matter how tough life may be that it is never good to quit.

Thank you God for the friend who made me see life can be a true, happy dance...
This one showed me that I do not always have to remain the victim of bad circumstance.

Thank you God for the friend who helped me find a way to really feel complete...
This one helped me see that I did not have to ever be resigned to accept defeat.

Thank you God for all the friends who have been my knights in shining armor...
Because they all loved me so much during my life that my heart and soul have become stronger.

Thank You for Teaching Me

Thank you for teaching me how to love.

Thank you for teaching me how to forgive.

Thank you for believing in me and showing me the best in life.

Thank you for letting me fall to learn from my mistakes.

Thank you for letting me cry so I don't have to let my sadness consume me.

Thank you for letting me laugh so I don't have to take everything so seriously.

Thank you for showing me how to say "thank you" so I never have to take one day for granted.

That Little Yellow Butterfly

That little yellow butterfly keeps flying close to me as I walk…
It's like it knows when I feel weak and too frustrated to even talk.

That little yellow butterfly often tries to keep me protected…
Somehow it remains my friend when I feel lost and rejected.

That little yellow butterfly knows exactly when to cross my path…
In its little mind it knows when I feel unbalanced and completely off track.

That little yellow butterfly likes to dance close to my trembling feet…
Within its soul it knows my spirit is really about to collapse in utter defeat.

That little yellow butterfly has a way of knowing when I really need a friend…
It's like it's the spirit of another life before me that never got to enjoy its life before the end.

That little yellow butterfly does not want me to walk alone…
It somehow knows when I just want to cry and hide from the world within my peaceful home.

That little yellow butterfly seems to flutter its wings in comfort when I really feel sad…
I can watch it for minutes when it reminds me God's beauty is more than just a passing fad.

That little yellow butterfly seems to sparkle in the rays of sunshine that give it light…
No matter how upset I may be, it seems to know when I'm just not feeling all right.

That little yellow butterfly never forgets to greet me with wings of joy…
Its God little message that it understands what it's like to live in constant turmoil.

That little yellow butterfly follows me in each direction I go…
I can feel its spirit reaching for me to keep the faith and not to lose complete hope.

That little yellow butterfly comes my way in many shapes and sizes…
No matter what the weather it remains true to life and free of deceptive disguises.

That little yellow butterfly remains my forever trusted spiritual guide of the great outdoors…
It helps me take a deep breath knowing that everything will work out for the best in my world.

The Angel's Cry for Help

I'm the Angel of Despair looking for a new direction...
I feel lost in the midst of a storm that keeps me isolated from protection.

I'm the Angel of Dark Nights hoping someone will feel my tearful cries...
I look deep within to see if I can find the right answers to my unanswered whys.

I'm the Angel of Pain feeling locked in a world of utter despair...
I look around to see if I will ever find true happiness anywhere.

I'm the Angel of Anger getting so mad I can hardly see straight...
I wonder why I always feel so misunderstood and keep making the same mistakes.

I'm the Angel of Guilt that beats myself up for not feeling I have done my best...
I long for the time I could sleep an entire night without losing moments of much needed rest.

I'm the Angel of Shame that cannot believe my life has not become what I had planned...
I just keep asking myself why it is I remain confused and feeling nobody understands.

I'm the Angel of Broken Dreams wishing at least something I needed could come true...
I'm so tired of halfway promises that just leave me sad and completely blue.

I'm the Angel of One Way Streets that seems to pick some of the most troubled paths...
I often look in the mirror and see why I have become the victim of destiny's wrath.

I'm the Angel of Confusion who never seems to know what choices I should make...
I just find myself feeling more misguided and feel one day it will be way too late.

I'm the Angel of Negative Energy fighting to maintain my own heart and soul...
I just can't find the strength to overcome the odds to fight and learn to be bold.

I'm the Angel of Faith crying out to help the dark side of my spirit bound in chains...
I just want her to realize that she truly is not alone to face her agonizing pains.

I'm the Angel of Hope ready to rescue the dark side of my spirit from utter tragedy...
I cannot imagine how I ever found my true self in the midst of her emotional misery.

I'm the Angel of Love ready to release the dark side of my spirit from a life that wounds her heart...
I long for her to learn that love and trust is all she needs to make a fresh start.

The Angel's Plea to be Saved from Psychic Vampires

I watch from above to see how the psychic vampires consume your troubled soul...
I know they have you so upset that all you want to do is just let go.

I feel your pain as these psychic vampires lean on you for your strength...
When deep in your soul, you keep yearning for someone who truly cares to be on your wavelength.

I whisper in your ears I know these psychic vampires around you causing you such pain...
If you keep clinging to their influence, your spirit will be tainted by much suffering and shame.

I feel the echo of your voice just wanting to break the psychic vampires' keeping you from rest...
I can feel you struggle from their grip as they try to suck the blood right out of your chest.

I surround you to let you know these psychic vampires will only crush your wounded heart...
All I can do is wrap my spiritual arms around you so you do not fall apart.

I see the mind games the psychic vampires play making you think they are really there for you...
Yet all they do is suck your giving spirit leaving you feeling like such a complete fool.

I send you peaceful dreams to somehow calm your most, unsettled fears...
Yet those psychic vampires send you nightmares and relentless tears.

I try to find a way to get you to take a much needed break from your worries...
Yet the psychic vampires entrap your soul with their own selfish, misguided stories.

I watch the psychic vampires wrestle with your mind through many sleepless nights...
My wish for you is that you block their energies to keep from feeling so uptight.

I feel the psychic vampires keeping you in constant emotional pain...
I feel they just won't stop until they have destroyed your honest, good name.

I'm the spiritual angel truly in love with your soul so much...
I promise to shield your spirit from these psychic vampires with my forever loving touch.

The Angel that Was Proud to Never Stopped Smiling

I was created by God to never forget to smile…
He loved me so much that He wanted me to make others feel worthwhile.

From the beginning of time I knew my path was destined to be unique…
I was blessed from birth with a heart searching for joy and a soul with good instincts.

I have searched the world over for a place to call home…
God blessed me with a loving family so I would never be alone.

In times of trouble I always learned to live a simple life…
I've known in my heart life can be tough and full of endless strife.

With each passing year, I asked God to give me a gift…
He said I blessed you with a precious smile to stay strong and to never quit.

No matter how hard my crazy days have tried to consume my loving soul…
God gave me children to love with great happiness and a heart full of gold.

I've learned through all setbacks that God could always save my heart…
My journey was meant to be sacred right from the very start.

There have been times my eyes have been filled with unstoppable tears…
I just kept smiling through them knowing God would always comfort my fears.

As I have watched my own children grow and become strong…
I just kept smiling at each of them through the good times and when their choices were wrong.

Through every season of life I have smiled upon my family everyday…
My hope is that they would always find eternal wisdom and never forget to pray.

Now my children have given new life to their own special kids…
I will keep smiling upon them with great love knowing they will always be missed.

I'm the angel of smiles God sent to take a spiritual stand…
I will always send guidance to those I love searching for meaning and a need to understand.

As I enter my new life in a world of eternal peace…
I promise to love my family and friends with a smile that will put their troubled hearts at ease.

I'm the angel meant to never stop smiling from now throughout eternity…
My wish is that my family will always feel my unconditional love within every memory.

The Angel that Would Never Quit

I'm the angel of light ready to embrace your soul...
I watch you from above hoping you will never let me go.

I'm the angel of peace hoping to light your way...
All I can think of is how I want you to welcome my love for you one day.

I'm the angel of joy sending rain of peace to calm your fears...
I can see through the facade of joy you portray to hide your secret tears.

I'm the angel of courage giving you the strength to fight...
I can always tell when you face so many long, sleepless nights.

I'm the angel of time wanting you to make the most of each day...
I feel you when things are not going well and you just want to run away.

I'm the angel of unity bringing you closer to your dreams...
I will always make sure the choices you make are much greater than they seem.

I'm the angel of smiles that can encourage you to face all of life's suffocating chains
I understand there will be times when you think you are too weak to overcome their pain.

I'm the angel of bright days that can really enlighten your path...
I can protect you with my armor from all this world's crazy wrath.

I'm the angel of new beginnings ready to help you take on this world...
I can feel your spirit drowning in the midst of this life's crazy turmoil.

I'm the angel of rainbows full of every color to give you direction...
I will make sure in every way you are surrounded by divine protection.

I'm the angel of change that sings in harmony with the shifting wind...
I let my cool breeze of kindness embrace your soul like a long, awaited friend.

I'm the angel of emotions that can make you feel like your life is true...
I will hold your hand through all the tough times and always be loyal to you.

I'm the angel of freedom ready to give you wings to fly...
I will set you free from your burdens so you will not be captured by the world's endless whys.

I'm the angel of a better path God wanted me to bring into your life...
I trust I can give you the courage you need to rise above your present strife.

I'm the angel that will not quit because I love you unconditionally so...
My heart beats in harmony with yours so that, near or far, I can never let you go.

The Astral Playground

There's a mystical place where we often meet to play...
It's where we rest our worries and create a brighter and more meaningful day.

There's a special dream that keeps us in sync...
It's a journey of like minds connecting with a strong spiritual link.

In the nights we travel to visit each other in a world of treasured dreams...
Our astral visits tell us there's more to our bond than on the surface what it seems.

Every magical evening you greet me with your ever present smile...
You hold my hand gently reassuring me that my life is worthwhile.

As my long, tough days come to another challenging end...
I close my eyes and picture a visit from you, my most cherished spiritual friend.

During the course of a day that seems to be the same old story...
I connect with your spirit and feel the strength of your love in all its glory.

When my internal worries take over my anxious, restless mind...
I picture the joy that links our hearts through all the special times.

Every chance I get to try and escape my turmoil and pain...
Your warm, comforting spirit keeps me on path despite my suffering and shame.

All the times I feel nobody really understands all of my desperate needs...
You send me peaceful energy so I know you will always appreciate my good deeds.

In each special moment the astral playground is our time to reach out heart and soul...
Memories of our times together gives me the courage to never want to let you go.

Over all the enchanting days and nights our spirits connect our hearts...
The unconditional love between us will never keep us truly apart.

The Balancing Act

Life is about the ebb and flow of change and sometimes it is hard to stay on track...
Forces of life we cannot change hurt us so deeply we try to understand the mistakes from the past.
Time and time again we wonder if we will always feel pulled in so many directions....
Sometimes we just need to feel that life will get better if we just let go of the fears that come from unpredictable rejections.

If we lean one too way long, we fear it could change everything that may not always be right....
Then we fear if we stay right where we are we may always feel anxious and uptight.
If we take a leap of faith, sometimes we wonder if it is the right course of action...
Yet the battle between the heart and mind can be the most difficult interaction.

There are times of distress when we think maybe things will work themselves out...
Yet all the craziness from the outside world can make us so crazy all we want to do is shout.
Many day and nights pass when we think we finally have the key to understanding all those whys...
Then just when we think we know the correct answer someone tries to hurt us with their helpless and draining cries.

We can often be pulled in a new direction that others may not comprehend...
Yet they are not living anyone's unique path so who cares if they ever understand.
We often wonder if just one person could just say thank you for all the good we do...
But the truth is there will always be someone taking us for granted and making us feel like an utter fool.

We think maybe time can heal the wounds of those who have steered us off course...
But somehow even when we feel better these people blame us and make us feel so full of remorse.
Life can be the hardest adventure any of us every try to ride...
We will always face battles that are hard to overcome because they are driven by hearts grown cold with pride.

No matter what comes in our lives, we just wish someone would tell us I appreciate all you do...
Sometimes all it takes is getting a thank you and feeling nourished by a fresh gesture of gratitude.
The ups and downs of life make the game of balance one that is hard for any of us to achieve...
Somehow we just have to keep the faith and know everything happens for a reason if we just believe.

There are all kinds of balancing acts we all must face...
Some of them are easy to obtain while others can make us feel like a complete disgrace.
There will be times the balancing act seems to keep our hearts and minds off center.
We just have to say a prayer of hope and ask God to keep out inner spirits strong, caring, and tender.

The Bankrupt but Healing Heart

I looked deep within and found a heart that was broken and confused...
It seemed weary and worn by all of the times it became the victim of unfortunate clues.
There were times this heart was so full of life and ready to embrace any new soul...
Then there were times it trusted so much it was attacked and left out in the cold.

When I looked a little further to see why this heart was beating so fast...
It was just so desperate to find a way to conquer life's greatest setbacks.
The times I could barely feel this heart beating at all...
It was just drowning in despair from being hurt so much and unable to answer God's call.

Sometimes this heart could face life's greatest times of celebration...
Then there were moments it became so withdrawn from all the constant rejection.
I thought I could just hold my hand over this heart and listen to what it wanted to say...
All I could hear was it needed time to heal instead of always wanting to run away.

With tears in my eyes I wondered what I could do to help ease its pain...
This heart just cried out that it wanted to grow stronger and not feel so ashamed.
I decided to take this heart on a walk into the sunshine that was so beautiful and bright...
Somehow I felt like it needed something to melt the darkness to bring it back into the light.

With each step I took I prayed God could help this heart come back to life...
I asked God to set it free from this world's constant strife.
It seemed as hard as my life had been my walk became much lighter and free...
I could feel this heart starting to beat louder and more spiritually.

As I fell to my knees and asked God what I could do to keep this heart complete and whole...
He whispered never lose your faith and believe that you can always trust me and never let go.
With a smile on my face, I knew that my future would somehow be better than my past...
I could finally hold my hand over my heart knowing God was healing it with a love that would finally last.

The Battle between the Heart and the Mind

Once upon a time there was a unique battle between two powerful spirits of life...
These two forces seemed to fight constant struggles to prove which one was most right.
The mind always felt he had the answers to his inner spirit's needs...
Yet the heart also tried to soothe his inner spirit with some more sentimental emotional deeds.

There was not a day that passed that the mind felt it was superior to all reason...
But the heart wanted its inner spirit to understand that love just happens no matter what the season.
The mind was insistent on making his inner spirit do exactly what he felt was the best action...
Yet the heart could feel the deep sadness from its inner spirit trapped in a world of expected reaction.

Some days the mind tried to make its inner spirit feel that it should follow the path most traveled.
Yet the heart could sense its inner spirit was totally frustrated and feeling lost in an apathetic battle.
In some trying times the mind convinced its inner spirit that all it needed was logic to survive.
But the heart kept crying out to its inner spirit you have to trust your feelings so that they never die.

When life was difficult and seemed too hard to make it through so many tough days...
The mind told its inner spirit to ignore how you hurt and keep pretending to be tough through a facade of happy ways.
When the heart heard the mind tell its inner spirit all of these lies...
She just begged her inner friend to be wise and not fall victim to living a life in constant disguise.

The mind often got tired of hearing the heart tell its inner spirit to have joy...
But the heart wanted its inner spirit to feel strong and know joy comes from surviving turmoil.
During times of the saddest moments the mind told its inner spirit, you are too strong to cry...
The heart just soothed is anxious soul with reassuring words to say that it is ok to ask why.

Through many changing seasons that passed year after year...
The mind felt it had controlled its inner spirit to act with no emotion no matter what its fears...
The heart often would cry out to its inner spirit you cannot live life without listening to my voice…
If you always listen to your mind, you could miss your chance for true love by making the expected choice.

The inner spirit was often so confused he did not know what direction to take...
He often prayed God would silence the chaos within so he would not make any major mistakes.
As this spirit tried to understand what God really wanted him to do…
He whispered the mind guides your intellect but the heart knows that true love is good for you.

With constant searching this special soul knew that God had sent him on a spiritual quest...
He just kept praying daily that God would should him how to know which voice was best.
Through many long days and nights feeling so upset and in total question...
This special spirit said God I need you to give me some much needed direction.

After a long period of struggle, this lovely soul finally felt a peace within...
When he listened to his mind he knew this was the most relaxed it had ever been.
As he was happy to finally have his mind much more at peace...
The brave soul held his hand over his heart feeling the power of love finally set all his fears free.

The Bird in a Cage

I'm the bird in the cage flying around in endless cycles…
Hanging to one side wishing I could keep from feeling so stifled.

I'm singing new songs hoping to escape the trap that suffocates my soul…
Wishing I never had to grow so old.

I look outside my bars to catch a glimpse of the world that engulfs me…
Only to find my feathers weakened by sheer inner misery.

I cling so close to the side of my cage…
Wondering if the visitors around me notice my inner rage.

I watch the people stop to tell me how sweet they think me to be…
Yet on the inside I'm struggling to break free.

I see people of all diverse ages and ethnic races…
Admiring me quietly using all their good graces.

Every now and then someone whispers a simple greeting…
Yet I find myself too lost to acknowledge the meeting.

Sometimes I see another sad face that looks down with tears in his eyes…
And I wonder if he notices my depressed cries.

There are moments I see couples walk by me hand in hand…
Yet I keep wondering why love is easy for them and hard for me to understand.

At times when the long days fade into the night…
I find myself more troubled by all my misguided choices in life.

During the darkest of nights, I fly around my cage in utter despair…
Wondering to myself does anyone really care?

In my dreams that finally calm my troubled heart…
I finally realize that my world has not completely fallen apart.

As I wake and face another day…
I find myself repeating my empty act as the troubled bird in that same old cage.

I'm the bird in the cage who watches the world pass me by…
I pray that my will to live surpasses my need to die.

I'm the bird in the cage like every trapped spirit looking for a new path…
I'm hoping to escape the world's ongoing wrath.

I'm the bird in the cage praying for a chance to fly free…
As the sunlight shines on me, I find God does have a plan for me.

The Broken Soul

I was once born with a soul that was whole and complete...
It seemed with the first breath I took I entered this world destined to overcome all defeat.
My whole life I felt like I was meant to embrace hardships as if they were part of my chosen path...
I could take on the whole world without any help and feel strong enough to not look back.

Despite my courage over time I felt like my life was on too fast a pace...
I prayed everyday that God would help me find the answers so I would not feel like such a disgrace.
I searched the world over to try and find the answers to all my whys...
Yet somewhere along my path I remained so troubled to hear anything but my heart's cries.

There were so many moments when everything I tried to do seemed to fall apart...
I can remember just crying myself to sleep wondering when I could move past my wounded heart.
Through the long days and nights I never seemed to really feel at peace or in harmony...
It seemed the strong soul I once had became weary and lost in a sea of forgotten tranquility.

It was all I could do to remember the moments when I remember feeling strong...
I had let all of life's worries trouble me so much all I could sing were the same old sad songs.
I have spent most of my life drifting from one road to the next...
It is all I can do at times to just hang my head up high when all I want to do is just rest.

I often wonder how we can come into this world with a soul not tarnished by life's pain...
I long for the days in my childhood when my spirit was free and not suffering in constant shame.
So many times I have prayed for God to help me overcome the stress that has trapped my soul...
It's like I wanted to reconnect with my true self before the world trapped me and never let me go.

There are so many chances in life that I should have taken, but I was too weak to stand tall...
I could feel within my chest that my soul was broken so much it was ready to take a great fall.
I wish that I could tell you that my struggle with being true has been easy for me to endure...
Everyday I ask God to guide my path and heal the broken spirit within me with a love that's pure.

I have learned that life is all about taking risks and hoping that the hard times will pass...
Each time my soul has been broken I just hang on tight to God knowing His strength will last.
When I pray for the courage to face all those things that I do not often understand...
All I have to do is look up and trust God to lead my journey by holding onto His loving hand.

The Butterfly & the Rose

Once upon a time there was a butterfly searching for a place to call home...
It flew everywhere under the sun until it was greeted by a lovely red rose.
In a field where everything looked dry and bleak...
This beautiful red rose stood tall among the grassy fields looking strong and able to overcome all defeat.

The butterfly knew in its little soul that it had been lost and looking for some direction...
It thought to itself I wonder if that little rose could give me a much needed connection.
As the butterfly flew upon the rose hoping to find some peace of mind...
The rose just opened its buds more widely so the butterfly would know it made it to the right place just in time.

As the butterfly calmly rested upon the little red rose that seemed so full of joy...
The rose whispered I will always be your friend through all your pain and turmoil.
In the midst of a lovely, summer day when the sky was blue and bright...
The butterfly just felt a serene presence coming from its new friend the rose with such love and light.

In times of great sunny days the butterfly always sought out the rose to be his most trusted friend...
Then one day things changed and stormy weather hit so hard it was like it would never end.
Even though the butterfly could have flown to another place to rest from the bad weather...
It just embraced the stem of the rose with such devotion that all of nature knew they were able to weather the storms together.

As the warm summer season faded into the crisp, cool season of Fall...
The butterfly knew it was time for the rose's pedals to fall...
Even though that butterfly loved the rose more than his own heart...
He knew that they were destined to meet again and be together always from the start.

When it came to winter and it was time for the rose to withdraw until it could bud again...
The butterfly knew that it had to have faith its friend would find him once again.
As the butterfly drew back into its cocoon to find new strength and a refreshed soul...
When spring came again, the beautiful red rose and sweet butterfly embraced each other with a love that would not let each other go.

The Caged Heart

There once was a heart that felt trapped and confused...
It was full of so much hurt that it could not get past all the lies and forever blues.
At times it would beat a little harder hoping someone would hear its call...
Yet in the evening hours, it found itself all abandoned and ready to just give up on it all.

In moments of stress this heart just had fought all that it could...
There were times it kept screaming out all I ever did was be way too good.
During all the fights and struggles to just survive all the chaos...
This heart could not find its way out of the raging waters of pain and loss.

With each beat this heart wondered how long it could go on...
It seemed it just was tired of not getting the chance to embrace a brand new song.
Sometimes this heart did not know when it would ever be able to heal from all its pain...
It seemed just when it was getting better, someone would break it all over again.

As the long days passed and faded into another beautiful sunset...
This weary heart could just not get past all the trying times and painful regrets.
During the dark of night when everyone was sleeping at peace...
This broken heart just wanted to die to be set free from all its sadness and misery.

In times of celebration when it seemed everyone else was having good times...
This caged heart fell out of step with life's continual flow of nice rhythm and rhymes.
Even when life was so tough for others that surrounded it so much...
This caged heart was just too frustrated to listen and felt like completely giving up.

Through the months and years that passed from one season to the next...
The caged heart thought I wonder when I will be set free and able to overcome all of life's tests.
With much despair, the caged heart could never find the answers it needed to truly understand...
All it knew was it had the love of God keeping it from faltering as He held it gently in His loving hands.

The Candle Whose Flame Could Not Survive

I was burning so bright when everything in my life was good…
I could conquer the world with the brightness of my flame when everything was just as it should.

I could light up a room in the darkest moments that always surrounded me…
I was the one everyone always turned to when life would end up in sheer misery.

Over the course of time, my bright flame started to grow slowly more dim…
It was like I could feel the weight of the world fill me with such doubts and forever sins.

Others would draw around me and could tell I did not seem as bright as I once lived my life…
I just could not keep burning with joy like I used to with all the worry and strife.

In the darkest of nights, I always tried to shine the most…
Yet I felt my loyal flame was being suffocated from intoxicating fears and painful ghosts.

Every now and then a harsh wind would blow my way…
It was like I could not keep my flame strong and felt myself melting slowly by the day.

As time has passed, my flame can barely stay lit…
It is all I can do some days to keep my spark alive when I would rather just quit.

When others walk by me they could not believe I had let my bright spark turn into a small flame…
I was crying on the inside you have destroyed my joy with your constant energy pull and hopeless games.

In the final days of my existence I wondered if anyone would notice my flame had finally died…
All I ever wanted was someone to just give back to me and be true without all the lies.

As my weary flame had burned out and nothing was barely left of my weary shell of a world…
I could see that there was nothing left to sustain this soul suffering in constant turmoil.

Now that my light has been put out with no spark left for others to see or feel…
I will never know if I was meant to live on to enjoy life or if dying was God's will.

All I know is some candles are hard to keep burning when all the forces of life try to dim its light…
I remain the broken candle whose own struggles put out my flame in the still of a lonely night.

The Cry of a Hungry Soul

A story exists deep within the hunger of our searching souls…
It's a melody of hope crying out for something to keep us from letting go.
A mystical song resonates within our hearts…
It's the voice of perseverance to keep hanging on when the good is out shadowed by the dark.

The winds of change blow unexpectedly each and every way…
They whisper a comforting solace to believe the good will outweigh the pain.
A storm of defeat tries to suspend us in a world hurt…
All we need is a prayer from above that life will get better if we just believe in a better world.

Sometimes what we can't control consumes the drive we have to do our best…
It is easier to give up than holding on to pass life's most challenging tests.
A faint cry is heard from a lonely bird flying aimlessly above…
All it wants is for someone to hold its wings to help it fly with an abundance of love.

A sunny, blue sky darkens after the brightest of days…
It falls asleep into a world of dreams that can empower our most difficult ways.
A fog of confusion wants to lead us off our most desired track…
Sometimes it takes faith in a Higher Power to lead us right back.

A journey of choices is something we are all expected to make…
Sometimes what we learn most is life is a learning process destined to keep our spirits awake.
A call for a new beginning rests within the very heart of our deepest wishes…
It has the power to cut through wrong detours to give us strength to have drive and vision.

Sometimes we need to have someone just encourage our dreams…
To understand that what lies within is deeper than on the outside what it seems.
Every soul hungers for a chance to be brought back to life in the most creative of chances…
It moves gracefully to a rhythm of life that is full of hope and joyful dances.

The Day God Took My Hand

I was lost and alone on a path that seemed too hard for me to walk...
I was being tossed by the wind with anxious energies that silenced my desire to talk.
The harder I walked the more I just wanted to give completely up...
Yet I kept hearing a voice around me say I love you too much for you to say you have had enough.

I fell to my knees wondering if I could ever get my life to the place I was always meant to be...
But somehow my heart felt caged behind a world of despair that kept me from feeling free.
In my great sadness I did not know if I would find the strength to ever be strong again...
Somehow I knew I needed to feel the comfort of a loving, spiritual, most trusted friend.

In the midst of my distress I just cried so much I thought my tears would drown my soul…
Then I felt the warmth of a spiritual touch with a loving energy too strong to let me go.
As I looked up to see where this mysterious touch had come when I needed it so much...
All I could see was an angelic hand reaching down from Heavens with such a treasured touch.

After all the painful memories from my past that kept me troubled and confused...
You reached for my hand so I could feel the essence of peace from a spiritual touch that felt so true.
Feeling so weak that I was not sure I could even get back on my feet....
You were the One who reached for my hand and pulled me up as if I had not been worn down by defeat.

Even though I was surrounded by so much fog that tried to cloud my vision to see your face...
I was meant to trust the guidance of your touch leading me out of the darkness into a brighter place.
I was feeling so alone and as if nobody could ever rescue my failing heart...
Yet you were the One holding my hand through this uncertain path right from the start.

I knew that my life had always been one full of much pain and regret...
But somehow Your loving, spiritual touch helped me forgive the past and truly forget.
With more hope than I had ever had in my entire time of existence...
You just held my hand with such a powerful, courageous force helping me overcome all resistance.

The day God took my hand is the day my life has never been the same...
Every moment I have been given air to breathe, You provide the strength to keep me sane.
The day God took my hand is the very moment everything changed for the best...
No matter how hard my journey may be, He gives my soul the power to overcome all of life's tests.

The day God took me by the hand will always be the day He helped me feel the loving touch of a caring, trusting friend.

The Day I Crossed Over to Meet the Kindred Spirit That Changed my Life

I was walking along the shore of a lovely beach far from my home...
I could feel my heart grow weary from being disconnected from my own soul that had grown cold.
As I took a few steps and watched the way my footsteps left traces in the sand...
I could feel a sharp pressure in my chest so painful that was too hard to understand.

Just when I thought I could ignore this hurtful feeling within my chest...
Suddenly I lost my breath and fell into the sand as if the very life of me had been put to the test.
In an instant I was being pulled through a long, black tunnel at such a fast speed...
It seemed everything around me was spinning so quickly I felt out of control and out of my league.

After my quick journey through the dark tunnel that carried me far away...
I was greeted by a being of light that said I want to know if your life was worth it in every way.
Confused and amazed I asked this being of light what I was meant to learn...
He said I want you to think back and trust me enough to tell me your highs and your hurts.

As I reflected on all the good times I had when I was a child...
This being of light cried I can see you always liked to run and play and never lost your smile.
When I remembered the times I had grown into a teenager with unpredictable moods...
This being of light said I hoped one day your careless lessons would eventually be understood.

I then explored memories after my high school years when I entered college to enlighten my mind...
The being of light said I shared spiritual truths each time you were led to read between the lines.
When I recalled my years after college trying to make my way into some sort of career...
This being of light said I was often the voice of reason guiding you to overcome all your fears.

As I reached adulthood and had spent several years trying to find my place...
This being of light said I sent so many people to help you discover good lessons along the way.
When I was being shown all the ups and downs my life had undergone in my adult life...
This being of light said I was always there sending you hope when everything was not going right.

After reflecting on my life up to this point in time...
I asked this being of light if there was anything I could do to have a second chance at life.
He looked right into the very essence of my soul and whispered I will always love you so much...
I said but we have just met so how could you love someone like me that you have never touched.

Suddenly this being of light surrounded me with such a bright light I could almost not see....
He whispered just listen to my voice and keep holding on to me.
As I closed my eyes I felt myself being pulled away from this other world of bliss...
Then I found myself back on the beach where I once lay wounded by broken dreams and stress.

As I awoke lying in the sand with a peace like I had never known...
I held my hand over my heart to find the pain that had crippled me finally left my desperate soul.
When I got back on my feet to raise my hands to connect with that being of light high in the sky....
I realized that he was my kindred spirit from the other side who had saved my life.

The Digital Embrace that Came Full Circle

From the day I was born, I never realized our friendship was so meant to be...
I went through most of my life feeling lost and beaten down with sheer misery.

From the time I was a child I grew up thinking trust was something for others to enjoy...
I just stayed alone and realized that everything I tried to do was truly in vain and lacking in joy.

As I grew older and encountered so many people I did not understand...
I asked God to send someone my way that would always be my most trusted friend...

The day God allowed me to be greeted by your warm, caring smile...
I realized very quickly that you could teach me my life really was worthwhile.

The time I spent sharing years of friendship with you was the best...
When I let you go years ago, I blamed myself for causing you such distress.

As many of the years passed, I asked God to give me a second chance...
All I wanted was to reconnect with you under the most encouraging circumstance.

From one simple message to another in the world of cyberspace...
I found once again that our souls remained connected with each digital embrace.

Every time messages have been exchanged between us in an online world...
All I do is thank God for the time to chat with you in the midst of my turmoil.

Some people come and go throughout all of our lives...
Yet my deep connection with you is the God given treasure that never dies.

I have searched the world over and looked deep within...
Yet I have not loved another like you so completely and fully from the day my breath began.

Every time I lay my head down to embrace another restful night...
All I do is just think of you and pray that you are truly all right.

When my days and nights linger so long as if I feel my life holds no meaning...
I just think of you and the past and realize God has a plan for a new beginning.

You are my most faithful friend and I ask you to forgive my forever wounded soul...
I still care for you so much that I cannot believe I ever let you go.

Please forgive me, my friend, for breaking your heart...
All I ever wanted was to love you forever and not tear your world apart.

As time passes and the long days and nights seem to never end...
I sincerely pray you hear me whisper so gently, come back to me my trusted friend.

The Divine Embrace of a Sacred Love Affair

I can feel you reach for me as much as you feel me reach for you...
I can accept the energy you send when you want me to know you understand my soul is true.
I can walk outside and wonder if the breeze I feel is your way of letting me know you are there...
I can reach into the sky and feel the angelic touch of your love letting me know you care.

I can search everyday to find some meaning in my often ordinary day...
I can see the ways you talk to me through special words spoken through strangers in unique ways.
I can listen to a song and feel your kind voice in the most harmonious melody...
I can dance in your light to the most inspirational musical symphony.

I can talk a walk outside exploring nature's finest creation story...
I can feel you speak to me through the freedom of a small bird spreading its wings in such glory.
I can look at a picture and see you in every color that makes it shine...
I can find your spiritual essence within a divine artwork that was created for your heart and mine.

I can feel all alone and wonder how I ever survived without you near my side...
I can sense in the darkness that when I can't find my way you will always by my guide.
I can fall asleep into a dream where only you and I create a mystical world of peace...
I can wake the next morning and feel you giving me strength to face a new day feeling at ease.

I can question all the ups and downs of my life and know you are there holding my hand...
I can always trust when the world feels crazy that you will always understand.
I can speak to your soul with a spiritual essence that nobody could ever touch...
I can feel that no matter where I go that you know I will always love you so much.

I can be strong and know that with courage nothing could ever keep us apart...
I can know the love that binds ours souls will keep us linked within the depths of our caring hearts.
I can feel the magical charm you so often send my way to make me smile...
I can just look into your eyes with a look of love that proves you make me feel worthwhile.

I can care deeply for your soul everyday for the rest of my life for all eternity...
I can move in sync with your spirit because together we share a magical destiny.
I can reach for your hand and feel you draw me into a warm, spiritual embrace...
I know in the depths of my heart and soul the sacred love that binds us will never go away.

The Dream Traveler

As I lay my head down to rest another mystical night...
The world of dreams send my soul on a journey into another life.

Thoughts of you spin round and round my mind...
I wonder if this dream will reflect another walk with you in time.

In one dream you are my protector and my friend...
The one encouraging me that all the hardships will eventually come to an end.

As a dream of sitting face to face with you comes into play...
You just smile at me and hold my hand so I don't go away.

In another dream you make sure you walk all the way with me...
The warmth of your presence sets my chained spirit free.

As the night progresses, I hear the spiritual messages you try to convey...
I wonder through your words if I can discover what you need through everything you say.

In the midst of my astral travels you whisper you will help me get by...
Somehow as you hold my hand I realize I don't need to keep asking God all the whys.

I know our time together is precious as we share space on the astral plane...
Somehow it's the only place we can truly visit without interruption and shame.

The night passes so quickly that I just don't want to ever be awake...
I'm desperate to keep you close so that my heart does not start to break.

When the night comes to another sad, quick end...
I struggle to keep sleeping to stay close to my most special, mystic friend.

As the light of day embraces my sleepy, weary eyes...
The dream of you remains the sacred memory keeping my spirit alive.

The Drifter and the Angel Hope

There once was a drifter who could soar through life without disgrace...
He was the king of his universe and the best at mind games to anyone's face.

This drifter knew when he could push the right buttons to make you laugh...
And in the same instance the Angel Hope could tell when he was just covering his internal wrath.

Some days the drifter would just pretend nothing could get him down...
The Angel Hope said I can tell when all you really want to do is hide that smile with a frown.

Many times the drifter felt he could charm anyone to get what he needed with his tricky ways...
The Angel Hope was always trying to cover his shame with much needed praise.

Everyday the drifter would think who can I fool who looks me right in the eye...
The Angel Hope loving him just held her head down trying so hard not to cry.

Once in awhile the drifter would notice that he felt empowered when acting fake...
The Angel Hope would cry out how many more hearts are you not going to break?

There were times the drifter would just sit back with a smug look knowing he was in control...
The Angel Hope would whisper in his mind why can't you just let go?

On cold winter days the drifter would just be happy everyone was feeling trapped...
The Angel Hope would cry out don't you feel guilty wishing harm on those in your path?

On days when blue skies and sunshine filled the sky with a calm, peaceful light...
The Angel Hope would see the drifter just basking in the darkness of his internal fight.

As the days and months passed before him, the drifter seemed to get tired of playing a part...
The Angel Hope just kept walking beside him knowing one day he would need her faithful heart.

There were moments the drifter would just lay his head down on his pillow with tears so strong...
The Angel Hope would lay beside him embracing him saying it's ok to sometimes be wrong.

In the mornings the drifter would stare in the mirror at his lonely, sad reflection...
The Angel Hope looked over his should and said maybe it's time to do some serious introspection.

In the next few weeks the drifter struggled day and night with what he really wanted to be...
The Angel Hope stood right by his side reassuring him that her love would set him free.

There were many sleepless nights the drifter just cried and slept with his hand over his chest...
The Angel Hope held his hand as he tried to erase the hurt he caused with his misguided quests.

As the time passed on, the drifter grew kinder in the way he treated others whose paths he crossed...
The Angel Hope just embraced him daily with great love that healed his wounded thoughts.

Now when the drifter needed to know all was ok...
The Angel Hope whispered I'm with you all the way.

The Emotional Roller Coaster Ride

There are some roller coasters that are always fun to ride…
They can bring you great joy and keep you flying so happy and high.
There are some roller coasters that seem to make you sick…
You keep wondering when they will stop spinning so fast so you will not feel you are a victim of a harsh trick.

There are some roller coasters that never seem to take a break…
It is like they just keep pressing so hard waiting for you to make another major mistake.
There are some roller coasters that always seem to go way too fast…
Before you know it all the good times fade too quickly and never seem to last.

There are some roller coasters that seem to go way too slow…
It's like you wonder when things will go faster or if you will ride the wave of the stagnant flow.
There are some roller coasters that have a way of breaking your heart…
It is like they keep you tossing and turning so quickly you feel your stomach remains uneasy from the start.

There are some roller coasters that have a way of making you think they care…
Then when you feel really safe, they just keep going off track and throwing you right into the air.
There are some roller coasters that go from side to side and never find a middle ground…
It is like they just seem to stop dead in their tracks wondering when they will find a more peaceful sound.

There are some roller coasters that have a unique way of being mysterious and deceptive…
Just when you think they are good to trust, you will find them far from being receptive.
There are some roller coasters that can take you to the highest mountain top…
Then others seem to stay right in the valley when you are feeling like you want to move but feel stopped.

There are some roller coasters that always want to take the easy way out…
Then just when you feel it is safe to let go, they leave you feeling lost when all you can do is shout.
There are some roller coasters that try to make you feel your ride together will be fine and ok…
It is because there are so many wolves in sheep's clothing determined to take your joy away.

There are some roller coasters that have a special way of making you never want the ride to end…
It is like your heart longs for a ride you can trust as if taking a trip with a long awaited great friend.
There are all kinds of roller coasters that are so bad and some that make you feel so good inside…
No matter what the destiny we are all meant to experience what life calls the inevitable roller coaster ride.

The Heartbreaker

There's a knife in my heart that just won't go away…
I feel that this sharp knife just crushes the very core of my soul every day.

There's a cold, bitter sword that pierces the deepest of my soul…
The negative energy of this life just will never let me go.

Many wolves in sheep's clothing tell me they care, but somehow I just don't believe…
Somehow I think my karmic debt is to remain in the dark isolated and deceived.

There is a pool of worry bound and determined to crush my mind…
I just can't escape the grip of despair that leaves me nervously tempted to be unkind.

There are whispers of darkness trying to break me down…
I just think I can't survive another disappointment that tries to run my heart right out of town.

There's a prison of misery that keeps me locked under the hottest, raging fire…
It burns deep within my soul like a wind that blows forever wild.

There are leaves blowing in a restless whirlwind around my heart…
Somehow I just can't move past the winds that have torn my spirit apart.

There's an eternal dream from which I just cannot escape…
No matter where I go the nightmares of life hold my goodness as a prize to be burned at the stake.

There is a channel of wisdom that I struggle to embrace…
I just am trying to understand why others attack me and leave me lost in a forest of disgrace.

No matter where I turn I've learned to give my broken heart to God who makes all things right…
He is the giver of healing and a spiritual destiny that keeps me going day and night.

The Heart of a Lost Soul

There's a heart that remains broken within the depths of a lost soul...
It's filled with an unrequited love that never seems to let it go.

There's a heart that beats with only half a lifeless measure...
It remains lost and broken in the midst of worthless treasures.

There's a heart that needs air to fully breathe...
It remains buried under years of disappointment and misguided deeds.

There's a heart that has loved and lost more times than then the grains of the sand...
It is locked in the mysteries of emotion that are so hard to understand.

There's a heart that tries to reach out in the valley of distress...
Yet it remains trapped alone in its own frustrated choices of struggles and disillusionment.

There's a heart that just cannot seem to find its place in a lonely world...
It is drowning on its own tears of anger and turmoil.

There's a heart that needs to know someone truly cares...
It finds the rhythm of life suffocated with madness and despair.

There's a heart that is caged by years of lost victories...
In the silence of the night it longs for solutions to life's miseries.

There's a heart that bounces with the ever changing tide...
It wonders how long it can hang on in the middle of life's crazy roller coaster rides.

There's a heart that yearns for some peaceful place to beat without disruption...
Somehow it can't seem to survive in the midst of challenge and continual corruption.

There's a desperate heart beating strongly in the lost souls of you and me...
It encourages us to walk our true path and embrace our spiritual destiny.

The Journey Back to Valentino

There is a journey that leads back to Valentino, a place where the heart calls home.

There is a path that leads back to Valentino, a place where the heart finds refuge from pain.

There is a destiny that leads back to Valentino, a place where the heart seeks courage for renewal.

There is an adventure that leads back to Valentino, a place where the heart longs for true joy.

There is a trail that leads back to Valentino, a place where the heart embraces beauty after despair.

There is a stream that leads back to Valentino, a place where the heart knows kindness flows.

There is an ocean that leads back to Valentino where the heart embraces seas of positive change.

There is a train that leads back to Valentino where the heart knows its choices are right on track.

There is a plane that leads back to Valentino where the heart finds freedom on the wings of hope.

There is highway that leads back to Valentino where the heart finds the right signs pointing to truth.

There are blizzards that lead back to Valentino where the heart finds warmth after times of cold.

There are stormy nights that lead back to Valentino where the heart finds nourishment for its soul.

There are hurricanes that lead back to Valentino where the heart finds comfort after troubled times.

There are tornadoes that lead back to Valentino where the heart finds rest after whirlwinds of anger.

There are tsunamis that lead back to Valentino where the heart finds solace after destruction.

There are clouds that lead back to Valentino where the heart finds its way through confusing times.

There are sunny days that lead back to Valentino where the heart finds great faith after dark nights.

On every path and during every season of life, God leads our hearts back to Valentino...
Where His strength never fails...
Where His peace never ends...
Where His pain is perfected in our weakness...
Where His struggle is our greatest comfort...
Where His tears wipe the very ones that stream down our faces...
Where His hope gives us strength...
Where His faith renews our troubled spirits...
Where His love mends our most broken hearts and embraces our most wounded souls...

There is a journey that leads back to Valentino where God loves you unconditionally and where the heart realizes the place that is its true home...heaven on earth...and paradise in the midst of struggle, the place that God will lead your heart back to in every way and through every season of life.

The Journey of Love Across a Thousand Lifetimes

I was standing by an ocean that seemed to pull my spirit to and fro...
It was like I could feel an energy pulling me back to another lifetime I had lived so long ago.
For some reason I could not remember anything as I stood there trying to understand...
Yet I could feel a loving energy embracing my spirit to try and focus on something that surpassed the time at hand.

I walked along the shore feeling as lost as I could be...
I looked into the Heavens and asked God where this powerful connection was taking me.
He said just have faith and let the breeze be your guide...
I promise you will feel a love you never lost that will stay forever by your side.

This journey I took was one I felt like I needed to embrace...
It was as if I was being led to find the other half of my heart despite my misguided mistakes.
When I took each step a feeling would come rushing over my mind...
It was like I could feel the touch of a special hand reminding me how I was always so kind.

I walked a little further and looked up to see a pelican flying through the air...
Then I felt a whisper telling me I was the one for you who always cared.
Intrigued by the warm familiar energy that seemed to make me smile...
I felt the ocean water wash over my feet as if it was telling me you always made me feel worthwhile.

As the waves continued to crash around my feet...
I realized there was a deeper energy I connected to that never let me give up in defeat.
Looking around to find a reason to keep walking this path...
I looked behind me and felt a familiar spirit encouraging me to not look back.

Taking the next few steps I found myself growing more and more weary...
It was as if a familiar spirit said I know your soul and can help you remember our heart's story.
Curious to know what I was meant to learn from this walk on the shore...
I felt a kindred spirit echo to my heart that the love we had was all I needed and nothing more.

Surprised and taken in by something that I was not sure I could feel...
A loving voice cried out to me that I was the one who loved you and always will.
As tears streamed down my saddened face...
I could feel a loving energy wipe each tear as if the life we had lived together had been full of grace.

After walking so long on this shore with the waves at my feet and the breeze carrying each step...
I could feel a familiar spirit inspiring me onward to keep the faith and not to give up just yet.
As I came to a place where I felt I like I needed so much rest...
I could feel a hand reach over my heart and whisper our love would never be lost in a world of regrets.

As I came to the end of my journey, I asked God to help me make sense of these emotions...
He just sent the spirit of a little seagull that felt like a long lost love who came right by my side with such loyalty and devotion.
As I lay in the sand this little seagull looked at me with eyes full of the most intense attraction...
I could feel the love of a thousand lifetimes still loving me deeply with such an eternal compassion.

The Leaves that Kept Falling

I walked along the path God cut out for you and me...
He whispered just keep on walking to each colored tree.

So as I took my first step, a tree dressed in a bright shade of orange caught my eye...
It blew right in front of my path and reminded me in my pain to keep my head always held high.

As I walked a little further another leaf dressed in a brilliant shade of yellow...
Came drifting before me to let me know it was ok to sometimes feel a little bit mellow.

On my journey through the woods a bright red leaf fell right in front of my path...
It seemed to keep blowing in front of me to shelter me from the world's crazy wrath.

When I continued walking, I noticed all the orange leaves fell right in front of my feet...
I could tell from their bold, vibrant aura that I was not meant to accept this world's defeat.

With every step I took I could tell all the golden, yellow leaves came into the mix...
It was as if I could feel their angelic healing energy protecting me from becoming so sick.

As my breath grew short and my legs weary, an entire group of yellow leaves in all their glory...
Just kept inspiring me to keep on singing new songs and telling fresh stories.

When it seemed I was too tired to try, the red leaves kept falling so quickly...
That I could feel great love coming to rescue my soul from despair so swiftly.

The Lighthouse in the Dark

I was lost at sea wondering if I would ever find my way out of the dark
I kept asking God when He would send an angel to help me mend from my wounded heart.
It seemed I had been swimming for so long I did not know which way to go...
I just felt I was tossing about on the waves of despair feeling frustrated with a soul grown cold.

In the midst of my sadness, I wondered when I would get a sign the darkness would somehow end...
I just kept crying out in the chaos of night wondering when God would send me a trusted friend.
It seemed the night grew long and I could barely hold my head above the troubled ocean...
I just felt the pull of the tide holding me back under the grip of painful emotion.

With a desperate spirit wondering when God would somehow help me find a way to survive...
I could not help but think I would rather drown in this water than live with my spirit barely alive.
No matter how hard I tried to swim to see if the shore of peace was somehow near...
It seemed I kept being pulled deeper into the turbulent waters that just increased all my fears.

I was so scared and worried that I just wanted to give up...
Then a voice cried from Heaven saying I love you too much for you to feel you have had enough.
Suddenly I knew I needed to swim harder to find a way out of this sea of lost tranquility...
I could hear God above say keep fighting and you will soon embrace a new place of serenity.

In a new spirit of hope, I decided maybe I needed to give myself a fresh new chance...
I could feel a spiritual shift that was pushing me to not lose the battle to any bad circumstance.
As the night grew long, I could feel my breath grow more and more weary...
But before I could close my eyes, I caught the glimpse of a lighthouse that had a brand new story.

All of a sudden I could feel life come slowly back into my troubled heart...
It was such a light of hope shining forth before me that I knew I was destined for a brand new start.
As I swam closer to the lighthouse that shined its light calmly on the waters before me...
It was then I knew God had healed my pain and brought me into His light of true love and harmony.

As I reached the shore that gave the lighthouse a firm place to stand...
I thanked God for giving me the chance to feel strong and hopeful again.
I knew God helped guide me to the lighthouse with no regrets or need to look back...
It was His light of protection that saved my soul with the lighthouse that got me on the right track.

The Lost Soul's Desire for a New Beginning

I'm the Lost Soul of Despair looking for a new direction...
I feel lost in the midst of a storm that keeps me isolated from protection.

I'm the Lost Soul of Dark Nights hoping someone will feel my tearful cries...
I look deep within to see if I can find the right answers to my unanswered whys.

I'm the Lost Soul of Pain feeling locked in a world of utter despair...
I look around to see if I will ever find true happiness anywhere.

I'm the Lost Soul of Anger getting so mad I can hardly see straight...
I wonder why I always feel so misunderstood and keep making the same mistakes.

I'm the Lost Soul of Guilt that beats myself up for not feeling I have done my best...
I long for the time I could sleep an entire night without losing moments of much needed rest.

I'm the Lost Soul of Shame that cannot believe my life has not become what I had planned...
I just keep asking myself why it is I remain confused and feeling nobody understands.

I'm the Lost Soul of Broken Dreams wishing at least something I needed could come true...
I'm so tired of halfway promises that just leave me sad and completely blue.

I'm the Lost Soul of One Way Streets that seems to pick some of the most troubled paths...
I often look in the mirror and see why I have become the victim of destiny's attacks.

I'm the Lost Soul of Confusion who never seems to know what choices I should make...
I just find myself feeling more misguided and feel one day it will be way too late.

I'm the Lost Soul of Negative Energy fighting to maintain my own heart and soul...
I just can't find the strength to be overcome the odds to fight and learn to be bold.

I'm the Lost Soul of Faith crying out to help the dark side of my spirit bound in chains...
I just want her to realize that she truly is not alone to face her agonizing pains.

I'm the Lost Soul of Hope ready to rescue the dark side of my spirit from utter tragedy...
I cannot imagine how I ever found my true self in the midst of her emotional misery.

I'm the Lost Soul of Love ready to release the dark side of my spirit from a life that hurts her heart...
I long for her to learn that love and trust is all she needs to make a fresh start.

The Mystical Love Birds

I was looking up to Heaven hoping to catch a glimpse of what true love really could be...
Before my eyes reached the clouds I saw two little birds sitting on a power line as cozy as could be.
I could not help but be drawn to the magical way they seemed to be so at ease...
My inner voice said just keep listening to them with an open heart and they will set you free.

As I stood watching these mystical love birds sing a new song...
I could hear one tell the other I will never leave your side but will make sure you stay strong.
When I listened a little deeper, I could hear the other bird say I will never let you fall from grace...
I was destined to love you from the beginning of time with unconditional love and kind ways.

As I listened closely, one bird whispered you complete my soul and keep me safe from the storm...
The other little bird said I will always be your faithful friend to keep you safe and forever warm.
I just could not take my eyes off these beautiful birds who exchanged words of love...
Just their calming presence alone was enough to feel a touch of divine serenity from God above.

I smiled at these birds and wondered if they had a message for me to hear...
One flapped his wings at me and said keep the faith because true love will conquer all your fears.
I asked the birds how they were able to discover a love so true and strong...
One little bird said we had to learn from other birds we thought were our soul mate, yet the choices we made were always wrong.

Intrigued by the very loving connection these birds seemed to share...
I then watched them fly away in sync in true harmony that seemed to echo in the air.
With tears in my eyes, I realized God did not want me to lose sight of forever love that never dies...
I could feel the spirit of Heaven healing all my hurts from the past with the touch of patience and time.

Every so often when I am down and out I will see these mystical love birds sitting in a park...
It is as if they want me to know that spiritual love heals our wounded souls when left in the dark.
When I just want to know that I must stand strong and not give up embracing passion and grace...
I can trust God's love will give me strength to fly like these mystical love birds with their wisdom and forever loving ways.

The One

You are the world to me.

Every breath I take is filled with warm thoughts of you.

You give me everything I need.

My heart is filled with the treasure of joy and peace you bring me.

You complete the other side of me.

I feel lost when you are away and yet when you are near, I feel whole again.

You are the one for me.

I could search this whole world over and never find another who enriches my life the way you do.

The Past Life Connection

I feel I have lived in so many other places and times...
Where life was much easier and full of a more peaceful harmony and rhyme.
In every life I lived you were always the one holding my hand through every defeat...
You could help me find the strength to rise above problems with courage when my spirit was weak.

In every life I lived I could always count on you as someone I could trust...
You carried my heart in in your hands when I needed hope and some good luck.
When I felt like nobody respected my feelings at all...
You were the one keeping me balanced when I felt like I was going to fall.

As decades have passed, I have played so many different parts...
Yet you came to me in the most perfect ways as the beautiful soul with the key to my heart.
When words could not express just how much you meant to me...
You could always smile with such grace that I felt in complete harmony.

In each life I found you so many people tried to keep us from being together...
Yet the strength of our connection was the binding force carrying us through all the tough weather.
In good and bad times you would never ever leave my side...
It was like you promised to be loyal to me forever throughout life's unpredictable rides.

Every life God gave me was such a beautiful gift of hope and love...
He promised to keep us together through all of life's despair under the protection of God's love.
Through every life when I would fall asleep into a deep dream...
You were right there encouraging me to remember that life not always what it seems.

From memory I remembered all the special moments in each of the lives we shared...
I could always feel you were the soul mate meant to be with me who deeply cared.
There was never a lifetime that I could not find you when I felt so lost...
You just promised to protect me forever no matter what the sacrifice or cost.

As I enter the present time where my life often seems broken and confused...
I can still feel your spirit around me when I need to feel an undying love that is faithful and true.
No matter where I go now or what choices I try to make...
You remain the lover of my soul with a dedicated heart and a loyalty that never breaks.

The Pelican Love Cruise

Once upon a time there were two pelicans riding the ocean waves on a crystal blue sea...
They were the best of friends who protected each other relentlessly.

During sunny days when the waves seemed to be so calm and at peace...
The pelicans just swam beside each other with a heart of love and a spirit so joyful and free.

As the morning gave way to another lovely sunrise that painted the sky with an artistic touch...
The two pelicans just glided over the water with such grace because they loved each other so much.

In the midst of very warm and bright sunny days...
The pelicans would often fly in sync in the most magical of ways.

Sometimes the skies would grow gray with stormy clouds marking the air...
Yet the pelicans just kept flying high because they could conquer the impending gloom and despair.

When the pelicans needed to find a safe place to land...
They just headed for the shore to find a nice place to lay their heads until the storm would end.

As the storm passed, the pelicans decided to ride the ocean waves in perfect harmony...
Their silent words of loyalty echoed their devotion to each other as the most powerful love story.

No matter how high or low the tides would rise and fall...
The pelicans were united through mind, body, and spirit as their destiny to be together would call.

There are Times We Think we Have Enough Time Yet

There are times we think we have enough time to say I am thinking of you...
Yet instead of saying you are in my thoughts, we remain silent thinking another day will be better.

There are times we think we have enough time to say I am worried about you...
Yet instead of acting on our worries, we just assume the other person knows we are concerned.

There are times we think we have enough time to say I want to help you...
Yet instead of trying to help, our good intentions go nowhere.

There are times we think we have enough time to say I will call you as soon as I can...
Yet instead of picking up the phone, we just put it off because we are too tired to care.

There are times we think we have enough time to say I really did not mean to upset you...
Yet instead of expressing these sentiments, we just minimize our response to anothers' pain.

There are times we think we have enough time to say I know you are hurting...
Yet instead of saying I feel your pain, we just say you will be just fine knowing the other person needs you to just take time out for them.

There are times we think we have enough time to say I know you are stressed beyond belief...
Yet instead of trying to help cope with the stress, we just act as if the other person is making too big a deal of his or her problems anyway.

There are times we think we have enough time to say I know you feel all alone...
Yet instead of saying I know you feel lost, we just assume the other person has it all together and does not really need our help.

There are times we think we have enough time to say I know you are tired and weary...
Yet we become consumed with our own agendas and neglect another person who just needs someone to be a shoulder to cry upon.

There are times we think we have enough time to say I am sorry and will you forgive me...
Yet instead of saying these words, we carry that grudge just a little longer.

There are times we think we have enough time to say I really do love you...
Yet instead of expressing what another means to our heart, we remain silent and the other remains disillusioned and heart-broken.

Life is short and yet timing is everything. Don't waste another moment wishing you had said or done something for another human soul because that one time you chose to hold back may be too late.

The Red Bird's Song

I soar the skies just looking for a glimpse of you.

I travel forest after forest hoping to catch you taking a walk to refresh your spirit.

I embrace clear, blue skies desiring to see your smiling face absorb the sunlight shining upon you.

I perch on tree limbs along nature trails waiting to hear you whisper hello in your soft, sweet voice.

I walk through green grass and colorful flowers so I don't miss your footsteps coming to meet me.

I fly from one tree to the next so that I can follow you and make sure you feel my loving presence.

I sing out loud hoping that you can hear me calling you closer to me so I do not feel so alone.

I break away from the other birds so I do not miss the way your eyes connect to my soul.

I watch you sitting by a creek of flowing water and make sure I fly to be near you in your silence.

I catch the kiss you blow my way and fly gently away because your love gives me strength to fly.

There is Always Someone

There is always someone who thinks he is much smarter than you...
He remains the charmer and spinner of lies that keep your thoughts distracted and confused.

There is always someone who thinks she took care of your needs...
Yet all she did was lie to your face and carry on with all of her misdeeds.

There is always someone who thinks he took the easy way out...
Somehow he made you think being authentic is not what it's really all about.

There is always someone that has a trick up his sleeve...
The kindness is just a facade she covered with deceitful intrigue.

There is always a game that someone likes to play...
He just smiles and whispers to his friend how he kept the lies going to get his way.

There is always someone set out to make you feel like an utter fool...
Then she just sits back and laughs knowing she played you and remained completely cool.

There is always someone who thinks she can pull the right strings to come out on top...
Sometimes all she had to do was make others fall down without knowing when to stop.

There is always someone who wants to make you feel and look like you are such a disgrace...
Sometimes he can charm you so much you forget real truth when it hits you in the face.

There is always someone who can talk a big talk and get anyone to believe her crazy games...
She has no remorse that innocent people have become the victim of her shameful ways.

There is always someone who makes a remark or two to make you look completely bad...
You feel the anger and he walks away smiling with no regret that you are so mad.

There is always someone who likes to think she knows how to manipulate your mind...
It does not matter what you need because she figures eventually you will give up in time.

There is always someone with a misguided plan...
Just remember life's misfortunes are not meant for us to understand.

The Restless Bird With an Undying Love

I'm the restless bird from another time and place…
I keep flapping my wings outside your window hoping you will let me feel your warm embrace.
So many times I sit alone wondering when I will always be on the outside looking in…
It seems the harder I try I still feel lost and at the whim and mercy of a relentless, cold wind.

I watch from the outside hoping I will find the courage to take a chance…
I am not the boldest bird because I have been a wounded victim of unfair circumstance.
I never know when I may catch a simple glimpse of you…
My faith in God tells me that one day you will feel the depth of how much I truly care for you.

I feel restless inside because I feel I am the bird always playing a part…
Yet inside my little soul I just want you to know I need you with all my heart.
Every day I sit calmly outside your window hoping it will be time to reach you on the other side…
I feel I am meant to be the one bird destined to make you happy through all times.

The rain of desperation falls so heavy on me at times I often do not know who I am…
It seems I am trying so hard, but God convinces me to quit trying so hard to understand.
As a new day begins, I keep hoping that I can sing a new melody to bring you joy and harmony…
No matter where I fly I will remain outside your window silently protecting you from insensitivity.

After sunny, bright days fade into several cool, crisp summer nights…
Somehow I know I love you so much because I want you to always feel all right.
I will flap my wings now and then because I know you see my soothing smile…
It seems I just feel connected to your spirit and cannot help but want to make you feel worthwhile.

I am not sure what God has destined to be for either of our chosen paths…
Yet I would do anything to make you feel secure and free from the target of other people's wrath.
You are the best part of me when I see you through outside the window of my soul…
I feel so restless deep within but inside the love I feel for you will never allow me to let you go.

I am the restless bird knowing why I stay outside your window with each breath I take…
The soul we share was a divine creation to keep our hearts strong and rooted in unwavering faith.
I am the restless bird who will always make sure you never are without a true friend…
On the outside I appear weary, but on the inside I will love you until my life is meant to end.

The Rhythmic Heartbeat

I held my hand over my chest and asked God to help me feel something truly great...
He said just keep the faith and the music you hear will bring you closer to your spiritual fate.
I listened more closely to try and feel the rhythm of this most precious tune...
He whispered if you hold on to the rhythm your heart will beat to a brand new start for you.

As I held my hand over my heart and listened to the music grow more harmonious to my ears
A magical connection bound me closer to my kindred spirit whose energy was free from fear.
I just let my heart drift softly into a new rhythm and rhyme...
It was like there was a powerful energy keeping me safe and in step with each movement in time.

I could sway one way and feel there was something special I needed to learn...
My heart grew stronger to a connected energy that had my best interests and highest concerns.
There were times I just thought this can be my greatest escape from it all...
I can lose my heart into a mix of high energy with a soul I trust that will never let me fall.

As each song played and I lost my current existence into a moment of complete bliss...
I knew in my heart there existed a world of truth where my kindred spirit and I could always exist.
In just a few steps I knew I would never lose such an unforgettable connection...
No matter what happened, I knew one day my heart with you would surpass all the rejection.

Amazed at how powerful God's mercy can truly be...
It was like my heart moved to a new rhythm of love that finally set my broken past free.
As I stopped to take the deepest breath my soul had needed for so long...
My heart would forever be connected to the kindred spirit who reached me with a spiritual song.

The Rocky Path

I was walking one day on a rocky path alone and confused...
I looked up to Heaven and asked, "God, I really need some divine guidance from You".

I walked with tears streaming down my saddened face...
I asked "God, why is it I feel trapped and cannot escape my troubled fate?"

As I continued my journey, my legs became more and more weary...
The tears became so heavy as I cried, "God, please take away all my suffering and inner fury!"

I wondered why God would let me continue to be so down and out...
In despair I asked Him, "Why can't I just be released from a life of constant struggle and doubt?"

As I continued my walk down this path full of broken rocks and weak branches...
My heart cried out, "God, why do I keep messing up all my second chances?"

I walked a little further hoping to see some light break through this muddy path...
My weakened spirit shouted, "How long will I be a victim of injustices and misguided attacks?"

As the day grew long and the night sky began to embrace the path from which I felt chained...
I looked up into the sky and said, "God when do you think You can release my pain?"

After a long day's journey I wondered where I could find a safe place to rest...
In my anger I said, "God, I really need one good night of peaceful sleep without any distress!"

I wandered on this path all night long not being able to truly sleep...
I prayed, "God, please let my soul not fall victim to a world of insomnia when I need peace!"

Hours passed and there was no rest for my weary, wounded soul...
All I kept praying was "God, I need You to hold me close and never let me go!"

As I reached the end of my journey, a crossroads of sorts greeted me with change and new starts...
In a moment of hope I cried, "God, I trust You to lead my by the hand and redirect my broken heart."

The Seagull and the Broken Seashell

There once was a lovely seagull flying above an ocean shore...
He felt lonely inside because he knew in his life he needed so much more.

Around him were people on the beach walking to and fro...
It seemed they were so full of life that the ocean waves did not want to let them go.

This little seagull would often ride upon the crest of a powerful wave...
He thought I wonder when I will find a true friend to carry me through all of my hard days.

In this moment this seagull knew he had to move forward from riding the waves of the ocean...
In his heart he knew he had spent lots of time surrounded by a ritual of lifeless motion.

The seagull thought and thought about what action he should take...
He felt if he stayed right where he was his little heart would continue to break.

As one powerful wave crashed right after the other upon the sandy beach...
He felt a pull to this one broken seashell that at first seemed out of reach.

As the little seagull flew to the shore to take a closer look as it lay helpless in the sand...
This broken seashell seemed it needed a friend to stand by its side that would always understand.

In one moment the seagull decided to wrap its wing around the shell's time worn stains...
Somehow he felt the shell needed a warm embrace that was free of hardship and constant pain.

As the day began to pass, the seagull decided to stand strong beside its new found friend...
This seagull would not let it wash away the shell at the request of the rushing water and harsh wind.

During the times the water tried to pull the seashell right back into the depth of the sea...
The seagull would pick it up and shelter it with the comfort of its wings.

As the continual tide and sunsets embraced the peaceful beach every day and night...
The seagull and seashell never left the other as they were united in harmonious love and light.

The Seagull's Cry

Some people call me crazy...others call me loving.
Some people call me adventurous...others call me cautious.
Some people think I fly too high...others think I fly too low.
Some people tell me I need to stay closer to shore...others tell me to do my own thing.
Some people walk past me on the beach with their loved ones...others just walk alone.
Some people try to feed me...while others just look at me with confusion.
Some people think I need to stay closer to those like me....while others tell me to be different.
Some people think I do not hear what they are saying...others can tell I sense things strongly.
Some people think I am a loner...others think I have too much heart.

Some people think I try too hard to be noticed...others think I need to try harder.
Some people walk by me with eyes of compassion...some look at me as if I am unworthy.
Some people think I need acceptance...others think I should not care so much.
Some people think I should fight no matter what...others think I should just give up trying.
Some people think I help others too much...others think I am too weak to help myself.
Some people cry when they see me standing alone...others just walk by me and laugh.
Some people think I am my own best friend...others think I am my own worst enemy.

Some people think I need to be more kind...others think I far exceed the limits of generosity.
Some people think I need to cry more...others think I need to laugh out loud more.
Some people feel sorry for me...others just think I feel too sorry for myself.
Some people try to make or break me...others are too wrapped up in themselves to care.
Some people think I am truly happy...others see me hiding behind a mask of utter despair.
Some people feel I am too hard on myself...others think I need to be harder.
Some people think I love too much...others think I don't love myself enough.
And some people just think they have the answers...when only God who knows me best.

To one person I am the seagull of freedom....to another I am the seagull of mystery.
To one person I am the seagull of playing it safe...to another I am the great risk taker.
To one person I am the seagull too afraid of courage...to another I am the symbol of strength.
To one person I am fearful...to another I have great confidence.
To one person I seem distant...to another I am nothing but your greatest ally.
To one person I am peaceful...to another one I am often distressed.
To one person I am discouraged...to another I am the great encourager.
To one person I appear the lost and lonely seagull...but to God I have never been unloved.

To others I am just a mere seagull...to one I am hopeless...to me I struggle...
but to God I am everything.

The Secret Language Between Kindred Spirits

From the beginning of time there was a secret language created just for you and me…
It was a message to stand strong and know we share the same spiritual destiny.
I could hear God whisper before I was even meant to walk in this world…
He told me I would meet someone one day who would comfort my pain and emotional turmoil.

I was thrown into a world where I often felt lost and confused…
He said just hang tight and you will meet your kindred spirit who will always believe in you.
Throughout my life's journey I have often felt nobody really knew me at all…
I thought I was meant to walk my path alone without knowing how to stand strong and not fall.

Through every season of my life I thought maybe my emotional pain would never end…
Yet God said just keep the faith and your kindred spirit will come to you as a most caring friend.
I could never really understand what God wanted me to know…
He said you have a warm heart but it is has been damaged by untrue spirits whose intentions have grown cold.

I searched the world over hoping to find the kindred spirit I knew God meant for me to meet…
The moment I looked into your eyes I knew you were the one able to conquer life's defeats.
During times when I was unable to share any words your way…
It was like just being in your presence was a sign from God that everything would eventually be ok.

As days and nights passed, I could often feel my weary soul reaching for your spiritual protection…
Just feeling the connection with you has given me hope in a world torn apart by lies and rejection.
I could walk your way and just connect with the magnetic ways you embrace each day of life…
Being my kindred spirit I know that you have a way of lifting me up when I feel trapped by so much strife.

I believe God gave us a mutual energy to share when the rest of the world does not make sense…
It is like there is a mystical world where we can escape to overcome all of life's chaos and suspense.
In the magical world we share there is no constant pain or sorrow…
We have a spiritual connection so strong that it helps give us strength to face every new tomorrow.

I know you can feel my good and bad days without having to ask me what is wrong…
In the depths of my heart, I know you hear the cries of my soul as if getting lost into a good song.
Through all the ups and downs that life often throws in either of the paths we walk…
We share a language of hope that surpasses other people's superficial ways and unhealthy talks.

God always knows when we are meant to find the kindred spirit that we can embrace in time...
He has helped us both overcome all the broken promises from the past and the hurtful lies…
No matter where I go or what this world tries to do to hold me back…
I can reach for my kindred spirit and your energy provides the balance to put me back on track.

We share a secret language that this world could never take away…
You are the kindred spirit I trust so deeply and will always cherish until my dying day.

The Shifting Clouds

I look above me and see the clouds gathering around in the midst of my troubled disguises…
I think somehow they see through the happy facade I wear to a heart torn apart by false surprises.
The more I look up I notice these clouds often change into so many unsettled forms…
It seems they are just as weakened as me when I have been through my own crazy storms.

I often see the clouds gathering around to protect me from all the despair that chains me…
It is like all the hardships of my past chase me down and rip my soul into an unfortunate mystery.
I take long drives hoping to settle the restless energy that often tries to rip apart my mind…
No matter where I go I cannot seem to escape the trap of being set free from my inner pain no matter how hard I try.

It seems that there are days the clouds often do not shift but seem at peace in a sunny, blue sky…
At times I just don't know what to do and wonder why I want to be happy but still cry on the inside.
I can rest my distressed body on a blanket of grass on a warm, spring day…
Yet the chaos in my spirit never seems to completely die but just keeps me paralyzed with a fear that won't go away.

When I look out the window up to the gloomy sky when the shifting clouds appear to grow dark…
I can feel they are about to rain down the tears of angels who connect with my troubled heart.
The rains come down so heavy that I cannot tell if the water is meant to heal or flood my path…
All I can do is fall to my knees and ask God to keep the stress of this life from bringing so many unexpected attacks.

The days and nights pass quickly and within every moment I strive to keep my dying spirit awake…
I wonder when the shifting clouds will show me how to keep from making the same mistakes.
Every day I look up into the clouds God created for me to find some level of peace…
I just pray in time that His wisdom will help put my suffering soul at ease.

The Snake on My Path

I was walking along a path when just by surprise…
A black snake stopped me right in my tracks as if he was a master in disguise.
In complete shock I tried to figure out what he was trying to say to me…
It was like he served as a reminder of all the tricks I had endured so relentlessly.

With total amazement, I tried to understand why he would stop me when life was going so well…
He said you have to face the past and face the hurts that kept you feeling lost and so frail.
I just shook my head and said I know I need to let things go…
He just slithered a little closer and said you have to face the pain before you are free to grow.

I felt my spirit getting so upset from this snake trying to tell me what to do…
He said he looked bad on the surface but always shed his skin to become strong and true.
I told him that he was a snake and why should I trust anything he said…
He let me know it was because my heart was halfway beating and needed love to be completely fed.

As I turned away to escape this creature that made me feel so uneasy…
He just slid closer and said you can't run from your fears because you will end up in a frenzy.
Somehow what the snake said actually started making sense…
I was so afraid he was going to hurt me but he understood my weak spirit and lack of defense.

Normally I would have run so fast away from something that scared me so much…
Yet this black snake had a kindness about him that cured the wounds within me I let nobody touch.
In a moment of pain, I wanted so much to just walk away…
Yet the sun shining on this snake convinced me he was sent from God convincing me to stay.

I looked up to the sky and asked God why he would send a snake to bring me a message…
He said sometimes life's hardest truths look deceiving when really it is a much needed lesson.
Confused I looked down at the black snake that would not leave my side…
He said God sent me to be your friend when the rest of the world has left you crying on the inside.

In fear I thought I needed to have faith that God is trying to help heal my broken spirit within…
Even though a snake had caused the fall of man, this one brought the chance to begin again.
I learned not to be too quick to judge something that God had intended for the good of my heart…
Sometimes it takes the most unexpected surprises to give us hope and a fresh new start.

The Silvery Blue Cord

There is a silvery, blue cord that connects you and me.
It gives me hope and it makes me truly happy.

There is a silvery, blue cord that binds our hearts and souls together.
It strengthens my spirit and keeps me feeling good during the most depressing days of weather.

There is a silvery, blue cord that keeps us both feeling alive.
It lifts me up and helps me know that you understand when I ask why.

There is a silvery, blue cord that keeps us in sync.
It makes me realize that we have a truly special emotional link.

There is a silvery, blue cord between us that will not be severed.
It gives me faith that the one word that will not exist between us is never.

There is a silvery, blue cord that is always the one constant we can trust.
It gives me hope that our connection is more than just a stroke of chance or good luck.

There is a silvery, blue cord that always is shining upon our dark days.
It gives me joy to know that your encouragement helps me in all ways.

There is a silvery, blue cord between us that can withstand all obstacles that try to break us down.
It makes me feel good to know that your undying support helps me stand my ground.

There is a silvery, blue cord between us that is spiritual and will never die.
It is what I hold onto when I pray and ask God to let me feel you when you laugh and when you cry.

There is a silvery blue cord that always draws you to me.
It is a powerful love that embraces our souls in complete bliss and harmony.

There is a silvery, blue cord that connects you and me.
And in my dreams, when our souls unite, God reminds us we were always meant to be.

The Snowflake Dance

I fall from the sky with white flakes fresh from the heavens above...
I cover your world with the softest array of purity and unconditional love.

I meet one by one my fluffy friends as we get ready to land in your way...
Trying to figure out if our attempts will give you a much needed break today.

I am often able to fall silently straight to the ground....
And hope that when you see me you will really take a look at your world around.

I cover your outside world with my white special magic...
Somehow my plan is that you'll see taking another day to relax is far from tragic.

I often can be carried away with the wind as it blows its chilly gusts right to your door...
When you step outside I hope I remind you to take a break from your usual chores.

I watch my other friends decorate your world with a peaceful glow of white...
Somehow I sense inside your soul you keep wanting everything to work out all right.

I see the tears well up in your eyes as your spirit cries out in pain...
I know in my quiet fall from grace that there is joy even when your soul is bound by chains.

I watch you struggle to get rid of all the snow that seems to stop you in your tracks...
Maybe if you listened to God this was meant to free you from your anxiety attacks.

I see your reflection in my calm, blanket of serene, quiet rest...
I want you to find some beauty in the moment despite your constant weariness.

I see your inside light often going dim without reason...
I just hope my purity wipes away your fears that keep you in despair every season.

I continue to dance with my friends in perfect, spiritual harmony...
Hoping that you take the time to see God loves you undoubtedly.

The Soul Connection That Kept Me from Falling

I was lost and confused, not sure of where I was being led to travel…
I felt like I was on a raging sea of chaos that attacked my soul leaving me feeling so unraveled.
No matter which way I turned I could not seem to find a safe place to call home…
Every place that used to matter to me now seemed empty and so alone.

I was pretending on the outside that everything was great in my often deceptive mind…
For some reason I could not figure out why when I was good to others they were so unkind.
I tried to figure out how I could find a way to start my life over again…
It was time I found a way out of all the battles I had lost to embrace those that would let me win.

Sometimes when I was walking against the fierce winds trying to blow me down…
I wished God would help me find a way to smile again to get rid of my unpredictable frown.
I often thought maybe I could stand on the edge of a cliff hoping an eagle would carry me away…
Yet I always stood forever while old problems still kept distressing me in the same frustrating ways.

One day I was walking down a nature trail thinking I could escape from it all…
Then I looked behind a tree and saw a little deer with such beauty I was in complete awe.
I stopped in my tracks just amazed at the peace this little deer seemed to bring my soul…
It was as if it was a messenger from God sent to remind me never to lose faith or let go.

As I walked a little closer to this deer I was afraid he might take off and run…
Yet the closer I got to him I could feel a peace come over me that warmed my soul like the sun.
This little deer just looked at me with eyes that seemed to reach deep within my heart…
I could feel an intense feeling of love from him as if he was meant to love me so I would not fall apart.

There were no words I could express to adequately reflect the love I felt for this deer I just met…
Somehow I felt he was carrying the soul of my great love who I was destined to love without regret.
The harder I stared into the loving deer's eyes the more I could see a reflection of the love I needed.
When our eyes locked together I could feel the energy of a love from so many lifetimes that never let me feel cheated.

I smiled back at this deer and watched him gallop with grace to another place to play…
His loving energy he left around me helped me know we would be connected in every way.
I remember that after I saw the deer that carried the soul of the one I would love with all my heart…
With every heartbeat I could feel the energy between us was too strong to let us ever drift apart.

Every so often when I need to feel the connection to the lover of my soul so much…
I can take a walk in nature and feel drawn to this little deer I came to love and was not able to touch.
It was like we had a language of love where our two souls could silently speak so calmly together…
The unconditional love between our spirits kept us feeling alive and always much better.

The Soul Mate Bird Outside My Window

I was sitting alone when a black bird outside my window seemed to echo the words in my soul…
He somehow wanted me to know how much someone loved me that promised to never let me go.
I could not understand why this bird had been sent on my path…
I felt God wanted me to feel the spirit of my soul mate in a bird who had escaped life's traps.

I watched him flap his wings as I smiled at him in complete harmony…
It was like he knew I needed a special friend to stand by my side through all eternity.
He seemed so restless that I could not understand why…
It was like he could feel my soul mate knew my heart was crying in such pain on the inside.

I looked up to Heaven and asked God what it was about this bird he wanted me to see…
He said I want you to feel the presence of your soul mate regardless of the outside world's misery.
My eyes became full of such emotions and tears…
Yet the bird just flapped its wings as if my soul mate was there to help me endure my fears.

There was something special about this bird that I just did not want to lose…
It was like he was my soul mate sent from God to say my spirit will always be true to you.
I was taken with the way this bird never wanted to leave the window sill that he had called home…
He just flapped his wings every time I looked at him saying he was the spirit of my soul mate and I would never be alone.

I sat and silently pondered what my soul mate through this bird was trying to say…
It was like he wanted me to know life would eventually become easier one day.
I knew in my heart that the love he carried for me was such a God given prize…
He would just flap his wings and said I am your soul mate in the most free-spirited disguise.

As I sat I watched him fly swiftly through the air…
I could feel him whisper that he was the link to the other half of my soul and would always care.
Just when I thought he might not come back…
He said I was sent by your soul mate to never let you fall off track.

There were moments that this little bird would always watch from outside the window glass…
I could feel my soul mate embracing my spirit through this bird with such devotion and class.
I know that there is a language of love spoken between soul mates that many do not understand…
This bird was the channel of hope my soul mate used to keep spiritually holding my hand.

The Soul Mate Energy Exchange

There was an exchange among equal spirits meant to cross each other's paths…
It was like destiny had meant for them to meet and take a new, fresh chance.
No matter where each one turned there was always quite a surprise…
The echo of spiritual music was the link that kept these souls connected through magical ties.

Days and nights would pass and there never seemed to be a time when either soul was alone…
As hard as life was their spirits were mixed together with a melody that never grew cold.
So many people could watch them from afar and never understand their connection…
There was such an unbreakable bond between them that surpassed anybody's rejection.

At times some people were so jealous of these souls because they had a language without words…
No matter how tough life was their souls were linked by the most harmonious rhythm ever heard.
Sometimes there were moments when it seemed that life really did not make much sense…
Yet these souls exchanged an energy of love that cut through all the careless hype and suspense.

During the happiest moments when life was not going great for one soul more than his friend…
The other soul could breathe a fresh energy of excitement to bring his soul mate back to life again.
When it seemed that life was just too hard for one soul to endure so much constant defeat…
The other soul could smile with such a magnetic force his soul mate felt able to embrace spiritual treats.

In the best of days when life was just not going quite as either soul had planned…
The soul mate looked right into his friend's eyes to communicate he really did understand.
When everything was on the right track for both souls to enjoy life so freely…
The energy of peace connecting their hearts kept their spirits together loving each other relentlessly.

In times when these souls were unable to be in each other's line of sight…
One could hold his hand over his chest and feel his friend's heart beating peacefully every night.
When the nights were long and it was so difficult for either soul to fall asleep…
Both souls could escape into a dream world where their energy drew them back together in peace.

During every changing season and through every problem that came their way…
The two souls loved each other so deeply that nothing could ever break their connection on any day.
In all the good and bad times when either soul just needed to feel a love that could never die…
The two souls exchanged an energy of promise to love and protect each other all the time.

The Soul Mate's Whisper

I whisper your name hoping you will come my way...
When I look around I feel you are the spirit getting me through the day.

I take long walks and catch a glimpse of nature's best surrounding me with such peace...
Knowing that somehow the negative energies around me fall away with your sweet release.

I close my eyes hoping that your gentle breeze can embrace my wounded soul...
Yet in the strength of the wind, I feel you holding me close and never letting me go.

I go through each day sometimes feeling so lost because I miss you so much...
You are the only one that always has the most loving spiritual touch.

I always try working at my job as best as I can....
And I feel you pushing me to keep going even when nobody else understands.

I find myself driving in my car thinking of how to handle life when things go wrong...
As the music plays around me, I feel your healing spirit inspire me with the right song.

I sometimes find myself lying wide awake at night finding it hard to sleep...
Wondering how you are doing and hoping you can send me energy to not feel so weak.

I awake each morning filled with lots of renewed courage and hope...
Because the dreams you send me are full of such love that I know I can truly cope.

I live each day feeling like the other half of my soul is missing...
Yet I know you are always there feeding my spirit with your thoughtful impressions.

As you whisper my name, I take a deep breath and hold my hand over my chest...
My spirit longs for you as I try to find the strength to endure life's challenging tests.

No matter what I do or where I go I promise to always be there for you...
Because your spiritual comfort is the divine treasure that remains loyal and true.

The Spiritual Bird that Protects My Soul

I was walking a path so few often want to travel...
My soul was feeling so restless as if it was fighting a constant losing battle.
In my search for meaning I asked God to give me a sign...
When I looked around me the beauty of nature was embracing my teary eyes.

Trying to find something that could ease my anxious heart...
I prayed God would send me something to ease my worrisome soul so it does not tear me apart.
I looked around me and was finally greeted by a little red and black bird...
It was looking down on me from a tree limb with the most precious eyes of loving concern.

I was curious about this bird and could not understand why it kept flapping its wings so freely...
The further I walked it just kept flying from one tree to the next to stay close to me.
Amazed at this little bird's determination to not leave my side...
I decided to stop and ask him what was so special about me that made him seek out my life.

The little bird never made a sound but flapped its wings with such peace and harmony...
I thought maybe this is the sign God sent my way to show me a different destiny.
For so long I was always trying to make everyone else happy when I was needing a friend...
Yet this little bird flying beside me as I kept walking wanted me to know true joy comes from within.

Every time I would stop to take a break...
This little bird would rest on a nearby tree beside me as if to say I know you want to run away.
Through our exchange of silent looks there was a loving energy the bird sent me to feel...
It was like he knew I needed to know that as hard as my life had been it was time for me to heal.

Even though I started my journey feeling so sad and downcast...
I knew with every step I took this little bird was God's way to say that the hard times would not last.
When I need to know that life will get easier to endure...
I can embrace this new path knowing the love from God will be the force pulling me through.

The Spiritual Love Between Twin Souls

From the beginning of time, there was a lost soul who felt all alone...
He kept asking God where is the missing link in his life to make him feel truly whole.
He said you will search the world over before your other half comes into your life by surprise...
Your twin soul mate will be the one with the greatest love in her heart that nobody could disguise.

With curiosity in his heart, the twin soul looked around to find an instant connection...
Yet all he found were broken promises from dishonest souls who left him drowning in rejection.
Downcast and discouraged, he wondered why he had to go through so much pain...
The twin soul prayed and asked God why He would let him love so many and yet feel disappointed and full of shame.

God told the twin soul to please not give up on his search for the other half of his heart...
He knew his twin soul partner was destined to rescue him right from the start.
One day before the twin soul knew what was about to take place...
He was drawn to the most beautiful soul he had ever seen who had such elegance and grace.

The magnetic pull the twin soul felt for this adorable spirit overpowered his soul...
He thought to himself could this be the one I was destined to meet before it is my time to go.
There was a powerful attraction that was so undeniable and true...
He hoped one day he could find the strength to be part of her world because he felt tied to her spirit through and through.

Despite the pull he felt to this lovely spiritual heart...
He knew there were obstacles between them keeping them physically apart.
No matter how many times he wanted to share more of his feelings when he got a chance...
He knew in his heart that he had to accept that a spiritual love without words was their greatest magic.

At times when his path did not cross the spiritual counterpart to whom he felt such devotion...
He spent his nights alone filled with thoughts of her and such loving emotion.
There were days he could feel when she was feeling so strong and encouraged...
And when life was not easy, he could feel her heart overwhelmed and discouraged.

At times he would just meditate and send her thoughts of love and peace...
Through her ups and downs, he wanted his spiritual lover to feel a calming emotional release.
There was not a day that went by that the twin soul did not think of his soul mate so faithfully....
He would always make sure he sent her loving energy so she would know he loved her unconditionally.

The twin soul had never felt a magnetic attraction that brought him back to life...
The presence and thought of his twin freed his anxious thoughts from day to day worries and strife.
As the days and nights passed, his heart and soul would never leave his soul mate's side...
The twin soul would love the other half of his spirit until the day he died.

The Swan Dance

You and I were made to dance in the midst of nature's finest tapestry…
We have a mutual melody of trust that surrounds us with great peace and harmony.
From the beginning of time, God knew that you and I were destined to meet…
Nobody in all creation could take away the trust that comforts our souls in the midst of defeat.

I have searched the world over and never found as beautiful a picture you portray to my heart…
It is as if the white feathers that clothe us were bound together with great love right from the start.
From the moment I first could swim gracefully across the crystal lake I call home…
God sent you as my dear little friend to swim beside me so I would never feel so alone.

Through seasons of winter when the snow and ice made getting around the lake so tough...
All I wanted to do was drown in despair but your support inspired me to never give up.
As winter faded and gave birth to the new life of spring…
I felt your energy giving me hope that life is more that empty promises and dormant dreams.

Even during times of spring when the rain seemed it would never stop falling…
All I had to do was reach for you and know that somehow I was meant to pursue a greater calling.
During the times the sun brightened the sky with strong rays of light...
You swam beside me from one end of the lake to the other reassuring me things would be all right.

As the spring gave way to summer's heat and most adventurous moments of surprises…
You just swam behind me to make sure I embraced my journey with no more disguises.
When the summer season faded into fall and colored leaves painted the air we breathe…
Al I had to do was look beside me and you told me I will stay by your side and never leave…

When the leaves fell upon the lake to color it with a fresh new look…
We could swim right through these leaves worn by the winds of change ready to start a new book.
As a new chapter in our lives unfolds with a new rhythm to dance to a fresh vibrant tune…
You and I glide across the crystal lake with a strong love my soul will always have for you.

The Tear Jerker

I looked up to Heaven and saw a rainbow of complete gold…
It seemed to be a sign from God to lift up my hands and never let go.
I looked around me hoping to find some peace of mind…
A voice whispered you got to hang tight through all the tough times.

I looked to my left thinking something might give me some sort of direction…
Before I knew what to do an energy shifted me elsewhere with a heart broken by rejection.
I looked to my right thinking this would be the correct way…
All I got was an echo of laughter saying don't trust what you see until you look for a brighter day.

I walked in circles trying to figure out what I was going to do…
Then the pain of darkness grabbed a tear or two.
I tried to hold back but something inside said you know you want to give up…
The agony of my lost soul was tired of being trapped in a sea of confusion and unhealthy stuff.

I tried to hold back the tears from cleansing my chest…
Yet something grabbed the tears so strong all I could feel was complete spiritual unrest.
I just could not believe that the tears would not stop streaming down my face…
I cried to God, "I know you love me but please make the tears stop and free me from my utter disgrace".

I watch my tears being jerked one by one so strongly I just felt weak and weary…
I fell down on my knees asking God to give me strength to have faith in the midst of my fury.
I could not stop the tears being jerked from my troubled, defeated eyes…
Then I felt the touch of an angel's wings that came as a welcome surprise.

I watched my tears being wiped away by the gentle touch of my new found friend…
It whispered God loves you so much that He took your tears to help heal your fears within.
I felt the warmth of the angel trying to catch the rest of my tears as they fell onto the ground…
It was not long before the tears stopped falling due to my smile that was no longer upside down.

I grabbed the angel by the hand and thanked her for helping me cope with so much pain…
It was the heavenly touch from above that gave me hope in the midst of my hopeless shame.
As I got up from my place of making some of my most difficult choices…
I decided to look above to hear the true voice of reason rather than a sea of misguided voices.

One by one my tears were no longer being jerked by a destiny I could not control…
I lifted my hands in the air to thank God for being the forever guardian of my enlightened soul.

The Train Ride of Confusion

There's a train ride of confusion bound and determined to consume my soul…
It grabs a hold of my heart so tight all I can think of is how can I let go.

There's a train ride of confusion running through the blood of my veins…
It whispers words of hope, yet I wake up frustrated for falling into another trap of deceptive chains.

There's a train ride of confusion keeping me a prisoner of many a sleepless night…
I wonder when I can sleep at peace just knowing that one day all my darkness will be overcome with light.

There's a train ride of confusion feeling my mind with racing, crazy thoughts of despair…
I feel my anxious inner spirit wondering if I can survive this whirlwind of chaotic nightmares.

There's a train ride of confusion always ready to keep me spinning in a world of endless chances…
I keep thinking back to the past when I could live life freely without worry and carefree dances.

There's a train ride of confusion trying to hold me back from spiritual victory…
I just wonder to myself if I will spend the rest of my life with my heart just lost in misery.

There's a train ride of confusion keeping me a prisoner to long nights of solitary confinement…
I keep wondering when the Universe will let my heart's desires come together in perfect alignment.

There's a train ride of confusion keeping me trapped in a life that seems dark and disillusioned…
I just don't know many times when to know if the truth is a facade of reality or just utter illusion.

There's a train ride of confusion ready to suffocate my soul from taking another deep breath…
I can see why so many people escape this life and just embrace a world of life after death.

There's a train ride of confusion going on so many directions I constantly lose track…
I just wish God would help me find my way before I reach the point of no turning back.

There's a train ride of confusion going so fast I do not think I can keeping it from derailing…
I just hope I can figure a way out of the maze to keep my heart and soul from completely failing.

There's a train ride of confusion racing through my mind…
With faith I pray to find the right answers in time.

The Unforgettable Soul Mate Connection

I was walking along a path trying to figure out what God wanted me to feel...
He said I know in your heart you have been searching for a love that is truly real.
I looked high and low and wondered where this love could be...
Then before I blinked my eyes there was a morning dove in my path staring right at me.

I tried to understand why it would let me get so close to it without flying away...
It just stood in peace sending such loving energies my way.
I walked a little closer trying to understand why it seemed totally without fear...
Then I realized it was trying to tell me it had a spiritual message I was destined to hear.

As I looked into its little eyes I could see that we made a connection...
After all my sadness this morning dove whispered I know what it is like to feel rejection.
I said how do you know how I feel when you are just a bird looking for food...
It flapped its wings and whispered I know what it feels like to be alone and feel confused.

In such amazement I asked the morning dove why he was all alone...
I said I thought birds like you fly in pairs so you can make it back safely home.
The morning dove claimed I am not like any of the other birds like me you have seen...
He cried I am the other half of your soul sent by God to protect you relentlessly.

I said how could you even know anything about my crazy, unsettled life...
The morning dove said I have watched you ever since you were young endure continual strife.
I looked at him and said how could you know anything about what I have been through...
Because I could hear your cries to God to have Him send someone who would truly be good to you.

With tears in my eyes, I cried how is it that you seem to know me so well when we just met...
The morning dove whispered I have been spiritually by your side through all of your regrets.
I said but why would you have been my side all this time without me knowing you were there...
The morning dove whispered after every time you prayed for hope you would see two morning doves, and I was always there showing you I care.

I could not understand why this morning dove was telling me all these things...
He flew closer and cried I will love you forever even if in this life you cannot always be with me.
I said I want you to tell me your reason for sharing so much of your heart...
I watched him fly away leaving his mark of love on my soul that had been there right from the start.

Every now and then when I want to feel the kind of love that soul mates truly embrace...
I can take a walk outside and see my friend the morning dove who greets me in special ways.
We may not always get lots of time to share the way we would like...
Yet when our eyes connect, the love that binds our souls lets us know we will always be all right.

The Unlucky Duck

There once was a lost duck swimming endlessly on a cool, crystal lake…
He said, "I wonder how long I will feel lost and totally frustrated by my forever mistakes?"
On a cool day in spring, he looked around trying to find one of his fellow friends…
It seemed the closer he got they all swam away, afraid they would have to be nice and make amends.

This unlucky duck thought, "Maybe I will find a safe place to just take a rest."
The more he thought, he felt, "Why is it I cannot find peace but a life of continual distress?"
As the unlucky duck tried to find some time to just swim away from his present place of pain…
It was like his poor little feet remained suspended in a puddle of struggle and unending shame.

When the unlucky duck finally found the strength to move on from his place of isolation…
All he could do was swim close to an island nearby that looked like a safe home free of desolation.
As the unlucky duck swam near the edge of a nearby island to find some food for his weary soul…
All he could think about was, "It would be so much easier if I could just learn to let go."

As the unlucky duck sat still looking at the island that he knew could him a much needed break…
He saw a little red bird in a tree looking down upon him with sparkling eyes free of heartache.
The little red bird began chirping with a melody of harmonious love and light…
In that one moment the unlucky duck knew that maybe everything would turn out all right.

The little red bird flew right down in front of the duck and flapped its wings with great charm…
It was like the unlucky duck had found a true treasure and a special friend to keep him unharmed.
He could not believe this little red bird was showing him so much love and devotion…
The unlucky duck knew that he had finally found a friend who was not afraid to show such great emotion.

As the unlucky duck decided to take a peaceful swim on the beautiful water in his midst…
That little red bird flew right by his side with a heart of gold that refused to let his good friend quit.
As the day faded into a lovely sunset that was magical and enchanted…
The duck knew his luck was changing because he no longer felt he would be taken for granted.

When the lucky duck swam back to the island to rest for the night…
The little red bird perched right beside him to give him forever comfort and a love that
would never die.

The Weary Path that led to a Rainbow

I was standing at the edge of the woods of life where all of a sudden two paths crossed my eye...
I tried to figure out which one I should take to keep from being held back by from all of my whys.
As I came to the fork in the woods, I felt led to take the path that seemed to be most chaotic...
I wanted to take the easier path, but the pull my spirit felt to the other one was simply so hypnotic.

As I began walking down this path, I was not sure if it would be safe from harm...
There were broken limbs and brutal winds surrounding this path worn down by false charms.
This path upon which I found myself so drawn was not an easy one to take...
I had to persevere so my heart would learn what was needed to grow through every mistake.

I found myself trying to escape the fog and scary creatures that would not leave me alone...
They just kept me living in fear so I would learn to trust that God would somehow lead me home.
After many long days and nights of walking this weary path I finally decided to give up...
I was in such turmoil and distress I knew that I just had more than enough.

In the midst of my despair, I asked God why He led me down this road of trials and tribulations...
He just whispered you had to travel a tough road to strengthen your soul in the midst of desolation.
I cried out this path is not clear enough for me to walk it with such confidence and pride...
God said you were meant to learn that life is not always an easy, fun-filled ride.

After so many years of struggle and running into so many obstacles on this path...
I finally realized I had to keep going and trust in God that I was not meant to look back.
Through the dark nights and the cloudy, foggy days...
I kept telling myself just keep the faith and you will discover it is going to be ok.

One day I just did not know if I would ever find a way out of so much of my pain...
When I wanted to give up, I saw a beautiful red bird flapping its wings with such love and praise.
This little carefree bird seemed to follow me relentlessly from tree to tree...
It was like an angel from God saying I will guide your steps if you just keep following me.

I decided to trust this little bird until I saw a colorful rainbow lighting the sky with its artistic flair...
All I could do was just thank God for sending me hope I had made it through all of my despair.
When I reached the end of this path, the colors from this rainbow greeted my soul with devotion...
I held my hand over my heart thanking God for leading me to a world full of loving emotion.

The Whispers of Love

Love in Disguise Whispers...
You know I love you...so make sure all your family and friends know I am the most important.
Love in Waiting Replies...
You know I really love you...so let your family and friends know they are always welcome at our door.

Love in Disguise Whispers...
You know I love you...so make sure nobody else gets close to you.
Love in Waiting Replies...
You know I really love you...so I want you to feel like you can talk to a true friend when at times it feels I may not understand your problems.

Love in Disguise Whispers...
You know I love you...so make sure I am the only one who gets all of your attention.
Love in Waiting Replies...
You know I really love you...so make sure others see just how beautiful you are to me.

Love in Disguise Whispers...
You know I love you...so who cares if you give up other people you care about just to be with me.
Love in Waiting Replies...
You know I really love you...so I do not want you sacrifice your loved ones because they are part of the life we have created together, and I want them to celebrate our joys and sorrows with us.

Love in Disguise Whispers...
You know I love you...so who cares if you are truly happy because I am all you will ever need.
Love in Waiting Replies...
You know I really love you...and even though I know I can contribute to your happiness, I also know there are other things in life than can enhance your joy too.

Love in Disguise Whispers...
You know I love you...so what is the point of crying when you are sad...you chose me so accept it.
Love in Waiting Replies...
You know I really love you...so when you cry, I will be there to wipe the tears or find someone who can give you the comfort you seek.

Love in Disguise Whispers...
You know I love you...so make the best of your life whether you are happy or not.
Love in Waiting Replies...
You know I really love you...so if at any point you find yourself unhappy, please let me know so together we can be strong and find solutions to your pain.

Love in Disguise Whispers...
You know I love you...so why do you get so upset at me when I just control the things I think you need.
Love in Waiting Replies...
You know I really love you...so why don't you just let me hold your hand and let you know that together we can make your dreams come true.

Love in Disguise Whispers...
You know I love you...so why do you think I isolate you from others because I will not lose you.

Love in Waiting Replies...
You know I really love you...so I want you to learn from others because there will be times I am not meant to show you all the things in life you are meant to learn.

Love in Disguise Whispers...
You know I love you...that is why I control you...that is why I isolate you...because I am your one and only, and I am the only one who will stand by your side.
Love in Waiting Replies...
You know I really love you...but I know I am only one person and even when I fail you, I still will be there for you and will allow others to help you when I am unable to be what you need.

Love in Disguise Whispers...
You know I love you...As long as you live in my shadow and do everything I ask, you will be happy eventually.
Love in Waiting Replies...
God created love and true love believes in you and has faith in you and leads you to the path of true happiness.

Love in Disguise Whispers...
Will you stop trying to confuse the one I love!

Love in Waiting Replies...
NEVER...Your love is built on empty promises and false hopes, but my love is God's love and gives my true love joy in the midst of pain and peace in the midst of turmoil. My love, dear friend, never fails.

The Whispers of the Wind

When the wind whispers my name...
I feel God knows I need a desperate change.

When the wind speaks to my heart...
I feel that God knows my world is falling apart.

When the wind embraces my soul...
I trust that God protects my weary body as it grows old.

When the wind hinders the next step I take...
I think to myself God is telling me I need a break.

When the wind tries to carry me to the next chapter of life...
I know God intends I learn from my strife.

When the wind blows so hard I can't see straight...
I know God wants me to learn how to truly wait.

When the wind roars so loud at night I can hardly sleep...
I sense God stays by my side as I weep.

When the wind gently comes in a soft breeze...
I trust in my heart God is healing my wounds with ease.

When the wind rips through valleys that haunt my mind...
I know there are answers God helps me find.

When the wind carries my spirit to great heights...
I have faith God always knows what is most right.

When the wind moves with the ocean waves to shore...
I see God leading me home to an open door.

When the wind shouts voices of praise...
I sense God telling me it will be ok in so many ways.

When the wind cries words of faith, hope, and love...
It is God's angels protecting me from above.

When the wind whispers its magic in so many voices...
I know I was meant to learn from my choices.

As the whispers of the wind bring a fresh start my way...
God remains my strength as I face another day.

The White Blue Light

There's a white blue light connecting you and me...
It shines strongly within the Universe to bind us completely.

There's a white blue light keeping us safe from harm...
It surrounds us with rays of hope and guides us with spiritual charm.

There's a white blue light keeping our hearts in total peace...
Its vibrant color brightens the darkness that keeps us from feeling so free.

There's a white blue light that never lets us wander far from thought...
It's bright spark fills our minds with a peace that could never be taught.

There's a white blue light that gives us wings to fly...
It's a source of strength that calms the tears when one of us just wants to cry.

There's a white blue light that shelters our spirit from pain...
It knows how brightly to shine to keep our souls from being torn apart with shame.

There's a white blue light that keeps the unspoken words between us protected...
It knows how to fill the gaps of silence when the world makes us feel rejected.

There's a white blue light that chases after our dreams...
It gives us an inner knowing that what is before us is never as good as it seems.

There's a white blue light that gives us nights of serene rest...
It provides the comfort needed when one of us does not feel our absolute best.

There's a white blue light that follows our hearts through every season...
It gives truth to despair when life becomes tough without reason.

There's a white blue light uniting us mind, body, and soul...
It holds the treasure chest of new beginnings that will never let us let each other go.

This World

This world may cause you grief…

Yet remember you can overcome all the obstacles in your way.

This world may make you angry…

Yet remember that others have walked in your shoes and there is someone who has felt your pain.

This world may make you frustrated…

Yet you must know that not everyone is against you.

This world may try to tear you down…

Yet you must know that there is always a light of faith to follow if we trust in God.

This world may use and abuse you…

Yet when you pray God will carry you through your adversities.

I want you to hold onto these words because I know my prayers are with you always.

This world is only temporary yet the world beyond us is eternal and you will survive this world.

Trapped

Trapped...by something that I cannot understand...
Yet yearning to break free from the chains that bind these hands.

Trapped...by a strange twist of fate...
Yet hoping to escape the binding force of something that does not feel so great.

Trapped...by moments that on the surface seem really bright...
Yet the air I breathe is consumed with anxiety that suffocates me at night.

Trapped...by words that hold no real hope or sincere consideration...
Yet I long to be encouraged with something true that sustains my spirit without hesitation.

Trapped...by charming echoes that at times seem to make sense...
Yet the words uttered become nothing more than false pretense.

Trapped...by false dreams that seem that they might come true...
Yet underneath the surface I feel like a powerless, hopeless fool.

Trapped...by misguided choices that end on one too many dead end streets...
Yet being pulled in a tricky direction that makes my spirit drained with deceit.

Trapped...by a desire to feel like someone that truly matters...
Yet all along my mind is confused and always too scattered.

Trapped...by a need to understand why certain things happen the way they do...
Yet knowing in my heart, God gave me the ability to understand what's wrong and what's true.

Trapped...by winds of hardship that try to break my heart...
Yet as the days go by I pray that God will keep me from falling completely apart.

Trapped...in a mirage of what seems the most delightful form of reason...
Yet the more I look inside myself, I find I have been a victim of treason.

Trapped...in a daily routine that seems to hold no hope for tomorrow...
Yet I long for the day I can escape the bondage of what seems to be perpetual sorrow.

Trapped...in a whirlwind that keeps me feeling there is no way out...
Yet my heart and spirit keep crying to overcome all my waves of doubt.

Trapped...by negative energy forces that disguise themselves as something so strong...
Yet beneath the surface I sense that something is truly wrong.

Trapped...by roadblocks making it hard to end my present state of worry and fret...
Yet hoping God will give me the energy to have courage to overcome my challenges without regret.

Trusting the Magical Love of Two Ducks

There was a time I wondered where my life was really meant to be…
I felt torn apart by questions I could not understand but hoped one day could finally see…
As I walked on an autumn day around a pond where the sun made the crystal water shine brightly…
I kept hoping God would help me see what true love looks like so I would not take it so lightly.

As I sat beside the crystal pond where I often go to find some sort of peace…
I looked up and saw two little ducks swim by me with such grace and ease.
At first it appeared the one duck was truly feeling so alone and lost…
Then as I took another look I saw his friend was swimming quickly to catch him at all costs.

I was amazed to see how fast the little lost duck found his forever, loving friend…
She just seemed to swim right beside him with the kind of peace that lies within.
Then all of a sudden the clouds seemed to cover the pond with a dark blanket of despair…
Yet the two little ducks loved each other so much they did not let the chaos around them suffocate their love and care.

The rain and storms came so heavy that day I barely could find a place to feel safe and ok…
My eyes remained on the two little ducks who made sure the storm did not get in their ways.
As tears streamed down my face, I could not believe just how happy each duck seemed to be…
During the rough waters they never lost hope because of the mutual air of trust God gave them to breathe.

I wanted so much to do something to help these little ducks get through the stormy weather…
Yet their love was so strong that I was amazed how they just stayed in the pond together.
As the clouds broke and the sun began to pierce through the gray skies to shine its calming light…
I walked to the edge of the pond where the two ducks had found a place to protect each other when all was not right.

In that moment of silence after the storm had given way to a time of great serenity...
The ducks looked up wanting me to not give up hope on love's forever melody.
Even though my heart had been saddened by so many past regrets…
The unconditional love between the two ducks reminded me to not give up hope just yet.

As I walked away and looked back to see where my feathered friends were going now…
I watched them fly through the air with wings of courage in a spirit of great love that would never let them fall down.

Walking the Path Back

I'm walking the path back to a time where life made sense...
Away from my present state of living that is drowning in constant suspense.

I'm walking the path back to a chapter where my life was more at peace...
A time when my soul spent more time smiling than being a victim of selfish feats.

I'm walking the path back to a time where life just seemed to fit...
A time when my heart felt a true harmony that just would not quit.

I'm walking the path back to days when all seemed right with the world...
A time when I did not always have to deal with constant turmoil.

I'm walking the path back to the moments that were full of lots of laughs...
A time I did not have to worry about dealing with so many other people's constant trash.

I'm walking the path back to nights that were free of never ending despair...
A time when I could escape the grip of others who truly do not care.

I'm walking the path back to special hours that were full of good cheer...
A time when I could truly relax and release so many of my fears.

I'm walking the path back to moments of celebration between friends...
A time when I could truly enjoy life without worrying how soon it would come to an end.

I'm walking the path back to a magical time where my spiritual path truly erupted...
A time when God gave me the strength to face future battles full of corruption.

I'm walking the path back to a time that was full of true connection...
A time when I felt I was truly at home and not feeling lost without direction.

As I walk the path back to a time where truth embraced my soul at all costs...
I'm reminded of the time when God blessed me with a spiritual love that would never be lost.

When the Thorn Fell in Love with the Rose

Once upon a time there was a thorn so disgusted with his life...
All he could think of was how he could just choke the rose that held him so closely day and night.

Everyday this thorn thought of how he had hurt so many of nature's best with his anger...
He did not care that his thoughtless actions had led to perpetual sticky dangers.

There were times when this thorn could not do anything but cause distress...
All he could do was think about when he could attack his next victim under emotional unrest.

Many times the thorn thought that his prickly nature could cause anything it touched great harm...
He knew that if he was tricky enough he could get what he wanted with his deceitful charm.

Some mornings he wondered when the rose he was attached to would somehow wither and die...
Yet everyday when he looked up to her red petals, all the rose did was blossom brighter and smile.

After all the birds and butterflies that came to greet the rose with friendly wishes...
The thorn could not figure out how they all went away with more uplifted visions.

During the night the thorn thought what can I do to kill this rose so it will quit smiling at me...
The thorn was also tired of nature's finest ignoring its sting and leaving it victim to its misery.

So one fine day the thorn looked up at the rose asking it why all nature was drawn to its red glow...
The rose just kept growing greater and stronger and just refused to let the thorn go.

No matter how many angry words and pain the thorn tried to inflict on the rose everyday...
The rose would drop a red petal onto the tip of the thorn so it would find some peace in every way.

As the sun would rise and set everyday and cast its shadows on the nature trail that gave it a home...
The thorn started to see that maybe it should be thankful the rose cared enough to protect its soul.

As the days passed and the season of spring continued to give the rose new life...
The thorn began to realize that it was not meant to live under the guise of constant strife.

When the light of day would pass into the stillness of a calm, peaceful night...
The thorn just kept clinging with all it had to the stem of the rose that protected it with great might.

Every moment that passed never seemed to stop the thorn from seeing the rose with a fresh spirit...
The thorn somehow found a peace that calmed its mind without all bad energies messing with it.

At the end of the fall, before winter came to put the rose to its seasonal rest...
Its petals fell on the ground one by one with such a delicate flow of peacefulness.

When the thorn looked upon the ground to see all that remained from the rose was the stem...
He just shed a tear knowing his good friend the rose loved him deeply until her life came to an end.

Whispers from an Angel in Heaven

When you hear me whisper your name, I am here to comfort your saddened spirit.

When you feel me look into your eyes, I am connecting deeply into your wounded soul.

When you feel me give you fresh breath, I am giving you a renewed sense of hope.

When you hear me reach for your hand, I am making sure you know I am here for you.

When you feel lost and alone, I will lead you to a safe place called home.

When you think nobody cares, I will make sure there is someone to comfort your broken heart.

When you think that nobody truly understands, I have been where you are and feel your pain.

When you hope to surpass your fears, I will give you the strength to overcome all odds.

When cloudy days come falling down hard around you, I will dwell in the midst of your sadness.

When it seems that everyone fights against you, I will always fight for you.

When you just want to quit trying, I will give you courage to persevere.

When you feel like crying, I will be there to catch your tears.

When you feel that someone is trying to bring you down, I will always lift you up.

When you look inside your soul longing to find what will make you happy, I'll be there for you.

When you search your heart for the answers to all your whys, I will say because I love you always.

There is a whisper from an Angel in Heaven calling your name...
I am God your father, your friend, and your great protector.

Afterword & About the Author

My name is Heather Dawn Wright, and I hope you have enjoyed reading my 1ˢᵗ book of self-published poetry called *Spiritual Whispers to the Soul*. I currently teach computer technology courses full time for a local community college in Boone, NC. However, my passion is in the areas of spirituality and writing. Because of these two passions, I felt led by God to create my own publishing company called *Colorful Spirit Publishing*, and I thank God for giving me the inspiration to write this 1ˢᵗ book. My dream is to continue writing more self-published books of poetry, nonfiction, and short stories that reflect the nature of human struggles and how through the spiritual world we are able to overcome them.

In a world where there is so much pain and suffering, it is nice to know that we can have faith in God and know He is the great healer and comfort to us when times are hard. Each of the poems in this book are reflections of many of my own hardships, yet through faith and perseverance, God has and continues to give me the strength to endure them. My hope and prayer is that He will give you the same courage and determination to know that there is spiritual wisdom to be discovered even in your current problems and to not lose hope that brighter days are ahead. I hope my book continues to touch your soul and gives you great spiritual insight as your lives continue to unfold.

If you would like to contact me regarding this publication or future writing projects, feel free to email me at hwright@colorfulspirit.com or visit my website at http://www.colorfulspirit.com.

Copyright © 2012 Colorful Spirit Publishing

Protected by freecopyright.org

ISBN-10: 098596331X

ISBN-13: 978-0-9859633-1-6

www.ingramcontent.com/pod-product-compliance
Lightning Source LLC
Chambersburg PA
CBHW081214020426
42331CB00012B/3029

* 9 7 8 0 9 8 5 9 6 3 3 1 6 *